Think on These Things

MICHELLE MONACO

CLAY BRIDGES
PRESS

Think on These Things
Copyright © 2024 by Michelle Monaco

Published by Clay Bridges Press in Houston, TX
www.ClayBridgesPress.com

Unless otherwise indicated, scripture quotations are taken from the (NKJV) New King James Version®. Copyright © 1982 by Thomas Nelson. Used by permission. All rights reserved.

eISBN: 978-1-68488-108-6
ISBN: 978-1-68488-107-9

Special Sales: Most Clay Bridges titles are available in special quantity discounts. Custom imprinting or excerpting can also be done to fit special needs. Contact Clay Bridges at Info@ClayBridgesPress.com

Dedication

I dedicate these works to my grandchildren, Michaelynn and George, who bless me more than I can ask or think. Also, to my daughter, a Proverbs 31 woman who is the reward for my faith to trust God and to give life. And to my son-in-law, who holds them all together.

–Michelle Monaco

Introduction

This devotional started out as a daily text to my grandchildren. I wanted them to get a little of God's Word in them before they started their busy days going to school. I knew they were not going to read anything that took more than a few seconds so, I kept my Bible quotes short and my explanations and exhortations down to a few sentences. Read one quote a day and think on it throughout the day. God will speak to you, "His word does not come back void."

I used the King James Bible and the New King James as my references to quote. I also used the Ryrie Study Bible and the Chuck Smith Calvary Chapel Bible for explanations and context.

Some of the wisdom that may be imparted here, I credit to the teaching of Chuck Smith, J. Vernon McGee, and all the anointed pastor's and teachers God has provided. Most of all, I give all glory to the Holy Spirit of God who is my teacher, counselor, who gave me light in my deepest darkness, wisdom amidst my folly, and boldness to climb out of the pit I was in and lead me into a new and wonderful life in Jesus Christ.

For anyone reading this, you cannot read these truths alone. Before you can glean any lasting good, you need to ask God, Our Heavenly Father to forgive you of sin, acknowledge Jesus' death as atonement, and invite the Holy Spirit into your life. Then, you will have eyes to see and ears to hear truth. You will never be the same. God will make you a new creature, and the eyes of your understanding will be opened. Try it!!!!

Old Testament

In the beginning God created the heaven and the earth.
Genesis 1:1

> When you believe this, you can have peace. God carefully planned, and you are a part of it. Thank God today that you were made with a purpose.

The Lord God formed man out of the dust of the ground.
Genesis 2:7

> We can believe this literally. The dirt is made of 17 elements, and the human body contains the same 17 elements. Isn't God clever?

Enoch walked with God; and he was not, for God took him.
Genesis 5:24

> This is one of my favorite scriptures. To think Enoch walked in God's will and His presence so closely that God decided to just pick him up and take Enoch home.

Come into the ark you and all our household, because I have seen that you are righteous before Me.
Genesis 7:1

> God spares those who are righteous from judgement. You are righteous if you gave yourself body, soul and mind to God. That's hard to picture. But pray each day to become more yielded to God.

Come, let Us go down there and confuse their language, that they may not understand one another's speech.
Genesis 11:7

> This was after the Tower of Babel. Building the tower to heaven may look nice but it was done to seek God on their own efforts and actually it was tied up with astrology. We come to salvation not by what we have done but what God has done for us. Differing languages may be to keep them from communicating these false beliefs.

Then she (Hagar) called the name of the Lord who sees me (El Roi).
Genesis 16:13

> Hagar was in trouble, pregnant and discarded by her mistress. But God spoke to comfort and gave her clear directions. God sees you too in your most desperate circumstances. Call on Him and wait for His comfort and guidance.

But Lot's wife looked back behind him, and she became a pillar of salt.
Genesis 19:26

> God granted grace to Lot and his family and let them escape Sodom before God destroyed this sin filled place. Lot's wife looked back with longing for this wicked place. She was not repentant.

And Abraham called the name of the place, The Lord Will Provide...
Genesis 22:14

> This was referring to where God told Abraham not to sacrifice Isaac and a ram appeared. Jesus is the sacrifice for our sin. God provided. We need only to acknowledge it.

Esau lifted up his voice and wept.
Genesis 27:38

> Jacob took Esau's birthright and blessing but don't feel sorry for Esau. He clearly did not value his relationship to God. Pray that you will not forget God's goodness, care, and privilege.

Behold, I am with you and will keep you wherever you go...
Genesis 28:15

> God spoke this to Jacob in a dream. Not all dreams are from God, but God does speak to us in dreams. God promises to be with you wherever you go that He leads you to go. God reminded Jacob of His covenant with Abraham to inherit the land.

Then Jacob was left alone, and a Man wrestled with him until the break of day.
Genesis 32:24

> Jacob was returning to the land of Canaan, but he feared Esau. He and God struggled, and God had to cripple Jacob to get him to trust God and not depend on his own devices. When the brothers met, Esau was kind. See? Trust God to do a better job at solving your problems. Go to Him and tell Him your needs and heart.

Put away your idols.
Genesis 35:2

Jacob was taking his family back to Bethel where he first heard from God, but they had other gods in their lives. Anything you give more time, more money, and thought to becomes your god. Make Jesus Christ first in your heart, soul, and mind (Deuteronomy 6:4-5).

The Lord was with him (Joseph) and whatever he did, the Lord made it prosper.
Genesis 39:23

By this time Joseph was sold a slave, put in charge of pharaoh's household, now imprisoned on false charges, he is given authority over prisoners. Next time you feel nothing is going right, think like Joseph; God put you there, He is good, stay focused on God and he will raise you up. He has plans for good and not for evil. (Jeremiah 29:11)

What you meant for evil against me; but God meant it for good.
Genesis 50:20

> Now look how this turned out. Joe's brothers tried to get rid of him, but God set him up to save their lives by providing for them in Egypt where he started as a slave. God has plans for you.
>
> Ask for guidance and humility each day so you can take the next step towards your future.

Moses' mother took an ark of bulrushes and put her baby in it...Pharaoh's daughter saw the ark...
Exodus 2:3,6

> You know the story. Moses a Hebrew was condemned to die but instead was raised by the Pharaoh's daughter. Now what are the chances of this girl finding baby Moses floating down the river? Take time to think of times in your life where God got you to the right place at the right time. Then give thanks.

I will harden Pharaoh's heart and multiply
My signs in the land of Egypt.
Exodus 7:3

> This is hard to understand. God told Moses to leave Egypt and then makes it more difficult because He hardened Pharaoh's heart. Ultimately God proved His power and might. Maybe He wanted to prove He is the God of the impossible. Don't give up. He is with us too.

Therefore send now and gather your
livestock and all that you have in the field,
for the hail shall come down on every man
and every animal which is in the field, and
they shall die.
Exodus 9:19

> This was God's way of showing mercy to the innocent. Pharaoh would not release the Hebrew slaves, so hail was coming to kill and destroy. Those who feared God and His word were spared. Those who love Jesus and live accordingly will be spared judgement as well.

The Lord went before them by day in a pillar of cloud and by night in a pillar of fire to give them light.
Exodus 13:21

God was not just leading but protecting them. We can get God's leading through prayer and reading His word. We are protected when we follow His plans.

Then Moses stretched out his hand over the sea, and the Lord caused the sea to go back by a strong wind that night and made the sea into dry land...
Exodus 14:21

When we obey God's direction, He makes it all possible. Back in verse 16 God told Moses to stretch out his hand. All Moses did was obey and look what happened. Not only did God remove the barrier of water but He even dried the ground so their feet wouldn't get muddy. Obey God and your path will be cleared and clean.

You shall select from all the people able men such as fear God, men of truth, hating covetousness.
Exodus 18:21

> God told this to Moses in selecting judges. This is good advice for anyone in selecting friends and prospective mates.

You shall neither mistreat a stranger nor oppress him, for you were strangers in the land of Egypt.
Exodus 22:21

> We hear so much about immigrants, but this can mean any stranger coming into your realm. Remember to be kind, patient, helpful in dealing with them. You may be the outsider one day.

You shall not circulate false report, follow a crowd to do evil, take bribes, oppress strangers,...
Exodus 23:1,2,8,9

> Now after Moses received the Ten Commandments, he reiterated these precepts to the people. They must be important. Let's ponder them and pray we not tempted to fall to these actions.

For Aaron's sons you shall make tunics and sashes...And you shall anoint them.
Exodus 29:40-41

Aaron and his sons were to be priests in the temple. They wore special clothes before going into the temple to remind them of their anointed appointment.

It would be good if we would take time each day before we pray or read God's Word to put on our spiritual clothes: the armor of God (Ephesians 6:14) and put on the Lord Jesus Christ (Romans 13:14).

And Moses said to Aaron, "What did this people do to you that you have brought so great a sin upon them?"
Exodus 32:21

While Moses was on Mt. Sinai talking with God and getting the Ten Commandments, Aaron was persuaded to create a gold god for the people to worship. Now these people were just led out of bondage, saw the Red Sea part, yet they did not recognize God. Are we that blind? Aaron had the responsibility as priest to say something when the people were led astray. Let's pray we speak up for Our Lord and point out His work to others.

Cut two tablets of stone like the first ones, and I will write on these tablets the words that were on the first that you broke.
Exodus 34:1

Remember Moses smashed the tablets when he came down Sinai and saw the people worshipping the gold calf. God is so patient and encouraging to us. He gives second chances and gives graciously when we blow it. There is none like Our God.

The people are bringing more than enough for doing the work the Lord commanded to be done.
Exodus 36:5

What gracious generous people. They saw the need for materials to build the temple. They gave so generously they were told not to give anymore. God's goodness should produce this same generous spirit in us. To give freely without reservation is a work of God's spirit in us. You can't out give God. What you give to Him, He returns one hundredfold.

...the children of Israel did according to all that the Lord had commanded Moses.
Exodus 39:32

> I pray we would determine to follow their example: keep your eyes on Jesus, pray about everything, and obey His commands.

No grain offering shall be made with leaven nor honey.
Leviticus 2:11

> This book of Law can be dry, but it is important. It sets up how the Jews were to sacrifice and worship. Before Jesus, the Law had to be followed. Leaven always represents sin as a little permeates the whole. Honey is to remind us we can't come to God by being sweet. We come to God through Jesus.

Do not drink wine or intoxicating drink when you go into the tabernacle, lest you die.
Leviticus 10:9

> This was instructed to Aaron and his sons who were priests. But we, too, should be set apart when we worship God and not rely on false stimulants. Be careful. No one knows if they will be an alcoholic or a drug addict until they take that first drink. It is best to stay away. Let the joy of the Lord be your drug of choice.

You, therefore, shall be holy, for I am holy.
Leviticus 11:45

> In this book, dietary law and rules for cleanliness for health are set up. Following these doesn't make you holy, but obeying God, setting aside what the world says is ok, and making sacrifice to get closer to God, does. Read these chapters (Leviticus 11-13). They make sense to keep healthy and free from disease.

You shall not make any cuttings in your flesh for the dead, nor tattoo any marks on you: I am the Lord.
Leviticus 19:28

> God doesn't want you messing up your beautiful body. This is what ungodly people did. You choose how you want to be identified.

If a man lies with a male as he lies with a woman, both of them shall be put to death.
Leviticus 20:13

> Now this is Old Testament justice. In Christ we have forgiveness, but sin is sin, and we must turn to Jesus for power to turn from it. Today people want to say gay is ok, but God has not changed His mind. We need to love these people and bring them to a saving knowledge of Jesus. Then, He can give them new life and power to change.

If one of your countrymen becomes poor and is unable to support himself among you, help him as you would an alien or temporary resident.
Leviticus 25:35

> Never look down on the poor, whatever the circumstance. God blesses us to set us free and see if we will be compassionate and give freely to those in need.

If you walk in My statutes and keep my commandments, I will give you (abundance, safety, peace blessings)
Leviticus 26:3

If you do not obey Me I will... (pour out terror, bring disease and sorrows.)
Leviticus 26:3,14

> Look at the choice here. As a young person, I didn't know how to follow God, and I made many bad choices. God has forgiven me and blessed me, but I suffered consequences of my poor choices for many years.

Take a census of the entire Israelite community...
Numbers 1:2

The book of Numbers lays out how important each tribe and each individual was to God. He assigned responsibilities to each. Do you know you have a calling on your life? You are not a random person to God. You were born for a reason. Daniel was a teenager when God called him out. Take this seriously. Ask God to show you your calling so you don't waste time on meaningless activity and disappointment.

The Lord bless you and keep you, The Lord make His face shine upon you; The Lord lift up His countenance upon you and give you peace.
Numbers 6:24-26

This was a blessing given by God. I wish nothing less for all of you. Receive it. Feel His light and goodness reach out to you. Stay in his gracious presence and you will have blessings and peace.

The ark of the covenant of the Lord went before them.
Numbers 10:33

As the Israelites were traveling from Egypt to the Promised Land, the ark was carried ahead of them to where they would camp. God 's presence is not carried in the ark today, but God goes before you in every situation making the way for rest, Follow His leading.

If the Lord delights in us, then He will bring us into this land and give it to us, a land flowing with milk and honey.
Numbers 14:8

The people have been doing a lot of complaining on this journey. Now they are doubting God's promise because of the giants they saw. If God is leading you, you will succeed but you may have to fight some giants (doubt, fear, hard work) along the way. Persevere. Keep your eyes on God not the obstacles. Trust Him and He will give you victory over these enemies of faith.

Bring Aaron's rod back before the Testimony to be a sign against rebels who complain against me.
Numbers 17:10

God set up this sign, the flowering of Aaron's rod, to prove to the complainers (unbelievers) that God had anointed Aaron to lead. It's tempting for us as well to want to follow our desires and not submit to God's leading. Have faith. His way is perfect.

Moses raised his arm and struck the rock two times with his staff. Water gushed out.
Numbers 20:11

That seems good, but Moses made a big mistake. God told him simply to speak to the rock. Because of his disobedience, he was not allowed to take the people into the Promised Land. Harsh, but God wants our total obedience and trust, especially as an example to others.

Now the donkey saw the Angel of the Lord with His sword drawn and the donkey turned aside.
Numbers 22:23

> Balaam was on his way to obey man rather than God. A donkey had to be the one to stop him from this evil. Let's pray that we have more sense.

If a man dies and has no son then you shall cause his inheritance to pass to his daughter.
Numbers 27:8

> This was radical in ancient times when women had few rights. But God made man and woman in His image. He does not put one over the other. We can respect each other and rejoice in who we are.

Your sin will find you out!
Numbers 32:23

> Moses gave this stern warning to the tribes of Gad, Reuben, and Manasseh. You can sin by not doing something if God tells you or by outward rebellion. Either way, you can't hide from God, but you can be forgiven.

*You shall appoint cities of refuge that a
man slayer who kills a man accidentally
may flee there.*
Numbers 35:11

God is gracious. Here He makes provision for one
who makes a mistake and another loses his life. The
old law would put him to death, but God distinguishes
between intent to kill and carelessness. We should
never feel we can't come to God to confess any sin.
He wants to protect and restore you.

*You must not fear them, for the Lord you
God Himself fights for you.*
Deuteronomy 3:22

This was instruction to Joshua as he entered into the
territories given him. God instructed him to go so
God would give Joshua victory. Don't be afraid to
take on challenges where God leads you. He will fight
for you too.

You shall love the Lord your God with all your heart, with all your soul, and all your strength.
Deuteronomy 6:5

So, there you have it. This is what Jesus said was the greatest commandment. Let's ask God to put this in our hearts and minds.

You shall remember the Lord your God, for it is He who gives you power to get wealth.
Deuteronomy 8:18

There is nothing wrong with working hard to gain wealth, but do it with a grateful heart. God gives us the mental and physical capacity to accomplish great things. He is the one who gives opportunities to succeed. Always be humble before God and man and give God thanks for all you achieve.

*What does God require of you but to fear
the Lord your God, to walk in His ways
and to love Him, to serve the Lord with all
your soul and keep His commandments, I
commend you for your good.*
Deuteronomy 10:12

Of course, you cannot do this until you know Him and
fall in love with our loving, heavenly Savior. It's easy
once you do. You want to walk justly, know mercy, and
humbly serve Him. I like the last sentence, "for your
good." God only asks us to do what will bring good
into our lives, not evil or despair.

*When you come into the land which the Lord
your God is giving you, you shall not learn
to follow the abominations of the nations.*
Deuteronomy 18:9

We can go into new situations, make friends, and learn
new things, but do not conform to what is against what
you know is right. Be ready to stand apart from the
crowd and stand up for the Lord.

God will not leave you or forsake you.
Deuteronomy 32:8

Moses repeated this to Joshua several times when he was preparing Joshua to lead the Israelite into the Promised Land. It must be important. Let's make this our mantra when we face uncertain times.

The eternal God is your refuge, and underneath are the everlasting arms. He will thrust out your enemies before you.
Deuteronomy 33:27

This is a beautiful promise. God is a refuge, a safe place to run in trouble. And if we fall, His everlasting arms will catch us. Our enemies will be brought to nothing.

Then Joshua, son of Nun secretly sent two spies from Shittim. "Go spy out the land,"
he said, "especially Jericho."
Joshua 2:1

Even when God gives you direction it is your responsibility to get information. Get prepared to do His work.

So the people shouted when the priests blew the trumpets. And it happened when the people heard the sound of the trumpet and the people shouted with a great shout that the wall fell down flat.
Joshua 6:20

This is one of the craziest recordings in the Bible. These people have been ready to fight, but God told them to march, blow a trumpet, and shout. The people obeyed this order beyond reason, and God gave the victory. Follow what God's Word commands, and you, too, will have victories beyond reason. When God's Spirit directs you to do the opposite of what you think you should do, do it. Don't try to do everything your way. Include God in your plans.

Then Joshua spoke to the Lord...So the sun stood still, and the moon stopped 'til the people had revenge on their enemies.'
Joshua 10:12-13

God came to Joshua's rescue after he called upon God for help. God wants us to ask for help so He can be glorified. Joshua needed more time to defeat his enemies.

Astronomers today still account for this two-hour lag when they make calculations. Again, science cannot deny God's control.

(The Lord said to Joshua) You are old. There remains much land yet to be conquered.
Joshua 13:1

This is true of us, when we accept Jesus as our Savior, we surrender our will. We are not immediately free of our old ways and desires. Sometimes it is a battle to "put off the old man" and become more like Jesus. But don't give up. God will give you victory to walk a life pleasing to Him. Focus on Him not your problem.

(Caleb) Here I am eighty-five years old. As yet I am as strong this day as on the day that Moses sent me; just as my strength was then, so now is my strength.
Joshua 14:11

We don't need to fear growing old. Age is nothing before God. (Psalm 39:5) His plans will be fulfilled in you and often your ministry doesn't start 'til you are older, (Exp. Moses, Noah, Caleb) Get going!

Not a word failed of any good thing which the Lord had spoken to the house of Israel. All came to pass.
Joshua 21:45

God keeps His word. It is good when we pray to use God's promises and pray them. He wants good things for you too and will bring them to pass. Look up His promises. God wants you to have plenty. Be joyful and glorify Him.

Choose for yourselves this day whom you will serve...But as for me and my house we will serve the Lord.
Joshua 24:15

Have you made that declaration? We can know who Jesus is and say thank you, but until you humble yourself before Him and set yourself aside to do only what pleases Him, you are not really saved. God wants your desires, thoughts, time, and devotion. In return, He gives eternal life, peace, joy, victory over evil, and success in all He leads you. Why wait? Ask Him to give that desire to have Him Lord of your life and trust to serve Him.

Another generation arose after them who did not know the Lord nor the work which He had done for Israel.
Judges 2:10

Wow! After all God did for these people, leading them from bondage to the Promised Land, they did not teach their children. God has no grandchildren. We each must learn of Him and decide if we will follow. Parents need to teach their children: talk of God, teach the Word, and pray with their children. Make God a part of your life. Don't forget all He has done.

The children of Israel did evil in the sight of the Lord and the Lord delivered them into the hand of the Midianites for seven years.
Judges 6:1

God uses our adversaries to deal with our rebellion. If we walk away from God, we reap what we sow: evil, injustice, hardship. Walk with the One who wants to bless you.

The people that are with you are too many for Me to give the Midianites into your hands...
Judges 7:2

How can there be too many soldiers to win the victory? God had Gideon send soldiers home and brought his army down to three hundred. God wanted the Israelites to see that it is God who wins our battles not our own efforts.

Put your trust in Him not your own strength or the help of others.

I have given my word to the Lord and cannot take it back.
Judges 11:35

Jephthah made a foolish vow to God. Yet, he kept it and sacrificed his daughter to fulfill it. When we vow or promise God, it is serious, but God does not want your sacrifices. God wants your love and obedience. "To obey is better than sacrifice."

But he did not know that the Lord left him.
Judges 16:20

This is the saddest sentence in the Bible. Samson was given a good home, super strength, an honorable position, and he gave to all up because he could not control his sexual desire. He chose three women who were not following God. Each one worse than the previous. He lost his position, eyes, and then his life. In the end God used him, but what blessings did he give up?

In those days there was no king in Israel; everyone did whatever he wanted.
Judges 21:25

This may sound okay, but we are selfish and imperfect by nature. The people were rebellious and didn't follow God's laws. They would need a leader to hold them accountable. We need to pray for our leaders even when we don't like them. This is hard but it does make sense.

Wherever you go, 1 will go and wherever you live, 1 will live; your people will be my people and your God my God.
Ruth 1:16

This quote is often used at weddings, but it is not about romantic love. Naomi and Ruth were both widows, and Naomi encouraged Ruth to return to her hometown, which was predominantly pagan. Ruth chose not to return but follow Naomi and accept the true God. God blessed her with a godly husband, children, and being part of the lineage of Jesus.

Do not boast so proudly or let arrogant word come out of your mouth for the Lord is a God of knowledge and actions are weighed by Him.
1 Samuel 2:3

God want us humble and wants our accomplishments to glorify Him. Remember, He is the one who gives you talent and abilities. Give Him glory and see what happens.

Who can stand before a holy Lord God?
1 Samuel 6:20

The answer is no one. The priest made sacrifices to enter the temple and even then, they feared. Jesus is our high priest and made the ultimate sacrifice for our sin. We just need to humble ourselves and accept it and acknowledge Jesus as our Savior. Then we can stand without fear or shame.

Then the Spirit of the Lord will come upon you, and you will prophesy with them and be turned into another man.
1 Samuel 10:6

Can people totally change character? The Bible says they can if the Holy Spirit is allowed to take control. God wants us all to be yielded to the Spirit so we too can be changed into a new man. A man who pleases God.

It pleased the Lord to make you His people.
1 Samuel 12:22

God chose you. He takes pleasure in your company. Spend some time with Him today.

To obey is better than sacrifice.
1 Samuel 15:22

This short sentence means much. Saul lost his position as king because he did not obey God and then offered sacrifice. We can say we're sorry, but true sorrow brings change. To obey is better than sacrificing our will and brings God's best.

The Lord does not see as man sees; for man looks at the outward appearance, but God looks at the heart.
1 Samuel 16:7

We all spend much time and money trying to look young and fashionable, but God is not concerned with that. He looks deeper into your heart. What do you value? What motivates you? Pleasing Him should be our driving force. Take time to evaluate your motives and goals. How does your inner man look?

So the priest gave him (David) holy bread; for there was no bread there but the showbread.
1 Samuel 21:6

> Only priests were allowed to eat this bread used for offering, but David and his men were hungry. Need supersedes ceremonial law. Compassion and kindness should be common sense.

Let the Lord judge between you and me, and let the Lord avenge me on you.
1 Samuel 24:12

> David spared Saul's life. He decided the Lord could deal with Saul better. This is good to remember when we feel like getting back at someone. Tell God about it. He will deal with it. You are His child.

Now the time that David dwelt in the country of the Philistines was a year and four months.
1 Samuel 27:7

> David was loved by God, but this is another one of his big mistakes. Having encountered Saul's advances twice, instead of getting God's direction, David ran to the enemy to hide out. There he falls into bad behavior. Trust God's way to direct and protect you. God will never guide you to rely on worldly methods to solve your problems.

But David strengthened himself in the Lord his God.
1 Samuel 30:6

> This is David's point. He had betrayed God and Israel. His own men stoned him. He could have despaired, but instead he repented and turned to God for hope and strength. You will never be disappointed when you do the same.

The Lord shall repay the evildoer according to his wickedness.
II Samuel 3:39

> Now David was grieving the death of his son Abner at the hand of Joab. He didn't retaliate or go after him. Instead, he let God take care of it. This wisdom, David displayed many times. It's good for us to remember this. God will get them.

David went on and grew great and the Lord of hosts was with him.
II Samuel 5:10

> In spite of all his failings, God anointed David to be king over Israel and the Lord gave him victory over the enemies. God will forgive us when our hearts are sincere and repentant before Him. No good thing will He withhold.

Is there still anyone who is left of the house of Saul, that might show him kindness for Jonathan's sake?
11 Samuel 9:1

Here we get a glimpse of who David was. Even though Saul relentlessly pursued David, David sought to be kind to his grandson out of loyalty to Jonathan. David was forgiving, gracious, and kind. Great character traits. Pray that God will develop these in you.

The sword will never depart from your house because you despised me and took the wife of Uriah the Hittite.
11 Samuel 12:10

OK. We know the story. David took Bathsheba, a married woman, and then killed her husband to cover his sin. First of all, you can't hide anything from God. Verse 13: "The Lord has taken away your sin." David was fogiven because he was repentant, but he had grave consequences for him and his family.

Then Ammon hated her exceedingly, so that the hatred with which he hated her was greater than the love he had for her.
II Samuel 13:15

Ammon professed love to Tamar and forced himself on her. Then he wanted nothing to do with her. This is the ugly truth of lust. Men and women should use discernment when letting their heart go. Don't be fooled by flattery. A godly man or woman will not lead you to lust or sinful behavior that will leave you empty.

The Lord lives! Blessed be my rock!
II Samuel 20:47

This is part of a song David wrote about his victories over his enemies. He gave God the credit and gave thanks and honor to Him. Think this day of all God has given to you. Sing out a thanks to Him.

He who rules over men must be just, ruling in the fear of God.
II Samuel 23:3

> This was wisdom from the Holy Spirit. I wish this were true of our leaders. Be careful who you follow and who you let influence your life. Let it be men who fear God.

Give to your servant as understanding heart to judge Your people, that I may be able to discern between good and evil.
1 Kings 3:9

May He turn our hearts to Him, to walk in all His ways.
1 Kings 8:58

> This was Solomon's prayer for the people at the dedication of the temple, and this is my prayer to you. Nothing is better than that.

Now all the earth sought the presence of Solomon to hear his wisdom, which God put in his heart.
1 Kings 10:24

> Don't forget where your abilities and gifts come from. Take time to humbly thank God. If you have the understanding, logic, and wisdom to follow God. Not everybody does.

Then the king answered the people roughly and rejected the advice the elders had given him.
1 Kings 12:13

> After Solomon's death, his son Rehoboam became leader. Instead of listening to the older advisors, he listened to his peer's advice on dealing with the people. The result was a disaster. The country split. Now, young people can have good ideas, but listen to what older experienced people have to say. Experience brings wisdom. If you heed advice of your elders, it could help you avoid devastating mistakes.

The ravens brought him bread and meat in the morning and he drank from the brook.
1 Kings 17:6

This was the beginning of Elijah's ministry. God taught Elijah to trust Him for supernatural provision. As a result, Elijah's faith was strong. He told the widow her flour bin and oil supply would not run dry is she shared, and Elijah prayed and brought back her dead son to life. When God leads you to step out in faith, He is preparing you for bigger things. Watch what He will do.

The Lord told Solomon he could ask for anything. This tells us how wise and selfless Solomon was. He asked for wisdom to be able to know good from evil. I suggest you ask God for this daily. It will surely make life easier.

The Lord was not in the wind, not in the earthquake, not in the fire, but a still small voice.
1 Kings 19:11-12

I shortened this, but read it when you can. The message is: sometimes we ask God, and we want a dramatic answer, but often the answer is right before us being revealed without fanfare. We're just not listening. Tune into God's voice by reading the Word, through prayer, and meditating on His goodness.

And the rest of the "perverted persons" who remained in the days of his (Jehoshaphat) father Asa he banished from the land.
1 Kings 22:46

> Judah had a series of good and bad rulers. Jehoshaphat was one of the better ones. He removed those who did not follow God's laws. Again, we are shown not to tolerate sinful behavior in our midst. Don't let yourself become complacent to immorality of any kind. Your heart will become dull to the Spirit of God. Which would you prefer in your life: sin or God's Spirit?

Then it happened, when the musician played, that the hand of the Lord came upon him.
II Kings 3:15

> Music is often referred to in Scripture. It is not entertainment but a powerful tool to prepare our hearts to receive God's Word. Music does have a way of touching our hearts. Make sure you listen to music that lifts your thoughts and heart, and of course, music which you can worship God.

Elisha cut a stick and threw it in the water where the ax head sunk, and it made it float.
II Kings 6:6

Now this is not displacement. The axe head surfacing was a miracle to show how God cares for details in our lives and provides for our mistakes. Next time you misplace something, ask the Holy Spirit to show you where it is.

So they went and called the gatekeepers and told them...
II Kings 7:10

Three lepers went out to check out the Syrian army and found evidence they had fled. The king did not believe them and sent out an army to discover the Syrians were gone. Unbelief will waste your time and rob you of the joy and blessings of God. Put your faith in His word and watch your life be enriched.

Joshua did what was right in the eyes of the Lord...however, the high places were not removed; the people continued false worship.
II Kings 12:2-3

> When you turn from your sinful behavior, make sure you eliminate all that causes you to return to it and all things that do not glorify God.

They did not require an account from the men into whose hand they delivered the money to be paid the workmen, for they dealt faithfully.
II Kings 12:15

> Money collected for the rebuilding of the temple was used to pay workers. These men who paid them were trustworthy. There is temptation to misuse money. Let's pray we are as these men; faithful and trustworthy.

...stay at home; for why should you meddle with trouble so that you fall?
II Kings 14:10

This is good advice. My dad would say, "Mind your own business." If a matter doesn't concern you, or you don't have the power to change things, stay out of it. It will keep you from trouble.

This disaster happened because the people of Israel sinned against the Lord God... They lived according to the custom of the nations.
II Kings 17:7-8

We should not be surprised as we see our country lose power and respect in this world. We, as a nation and as individuals, have accepted immoral standards and customs of the world that glorify immoral sex, lying, and cheating as acceptable. Let's pray we haven't gone too far. Each of us needs to stand up for righteousness. Speak the truth in love. Don't go down to the low standards that make you fit in. Stand out!

I have heard your prayer; I have seen your tears; surely, I will heal you.
II Kings 20:5

Hezekiah was given a grim diagnosis, but he prayed to God, and God gave him fifteen more years to live. Not everyone who prays for healing receives it. But always pray, "If it's God's will." God is still doing miracles.

When the king heard the words of the Book of the Law he tore his clothes.
II Kings 22:11

Josiah was a good king. When he read God's Word, he was overwhelmed with the holiness of God and how the people transgressed. He turned things around for the people by ridding the land of idols. When you finally experience God's holiness, you can no longer accept sin in your life. True repentance takes place.

I Chronicles 1-3

These chapters list the genealogies from Adam to David. You were not a random accident. God placed you in your family for a purpose: to bring Him glory and bless those in your family.

Oh, that you may bless me indeed, enlarge my territory, that your hand would be with me, and you would be with me, and you would keep me from evil and that I would not cause pain.
I Chronicles 4:10

Next to the Lord's Prayer, this is a good prayer to pray daily. Jabez is the author. He asked God:

1. To bless him
2. To increase his influence for good
3. To guide him
4. To keep him from evil influence and that he would not hurt anyone.

Jabez called to God, "Oh, that you would bless me, and enlarge my territory, that your hand would be with me, and keep me from evil, and that I may not cause pain.
I Chronicles 4:10

This is a good prayer. Ask God to bless you, give you more influence to do good, keep you from evil, and from hurting others. Try praying this and see what happens.

They cried out to God in battle. He heeded their prayer, because they put their trust in Him.
1 Chronicles 5:20

> I don't think this was a lengthy prayer, "in the midst of battle," but it was sincere. God honored their faith. Put your trust in Him. Call on God for help. He will answer. Your faith and trust will grow.

Now these are the men whom David appointed over the service of song in the house of the Lord.
1 Chronicles 6:31

> We see how important music is in the worship of God. Make room to listen to Christian music each day and let your heart worship. This will lift your thoughts and give you joy.

But Judah was carried away captive to Babylon because of their unfaithfulness.
1 Chronicles 9:1

Sometimes God uses our enemies to teach us a lesson.

So Saul died for his unfaithfulness which he committed against the Lord.
1 Chronicles 10:13

We are not punished because of our sin but we don't come into all God has for us.

David inquired again of God...
1 Chronicles 14:14

That word "again" is important. David didn't just pray once about this matter but each step of the way. Keep asking for guidance and keep listening for guidance.

Give to the Lord the glory due His name.
1 Chronicles 16:29

How can we not praise Him and give Him glory for what He has done in each of our lives!

Be of good courage...and may the Lord do what is good in His sight.
1 Chronicles 19:13

> If you are doing your best, God will be pleased and reward you. You don't need the praise of man.

Set your heart and your soul to seek the Lord your God.
1 Chronicles 22:19

> These were David's words to Solomon when getting ready to build the temple. This is good advice before attempting to work. "Seek the Lord's will."

The people rejoiced for they offered willingly with a willing heart to the Lord.
1 Chronicles 29:9

> It feels good to be generous and give to others especially when you know God has put it on your heart. That is what brings joy and rejoicing.

Because the Lord loves His people, He has made you king over them.
II Chronicles 2:11

> Hiram said this to Solomon. What a compliment. I hope we can be people God trusts to lead people in godly ways.

If my people who are called by My name, will humble themselves and pray seek My face and turn from their wicked ways, then I will hear from heaven and forgive their sins and heal their land.
II Chronicles 7:14

> Do you want your prayers answered? You need to come before God humbly and repent. Too often we think we can just ask God for help without true repentance. It's often our pride and disobedience that get us into trouble.

If you speak kind to these people and please them, and speak good words to them, they will be your servants forever.
II Chronicles 10:7

> This is good advice for all of us. Kindness wins friends, dissolves anger, and makes us better for it. God wants us to be kind to each other and everyone we encounter. Being kind makes us feel better too.

The Lord is with you while you are with Him.
II Chronicles 15:2

> God will protect, guide, and bless you as long as you want Him to, but if you want to live without Him and do not follow His teaching, you can.

For the eyes of the Lord run to and fro throughout the whole earth, to show Himself strong on behalf of those whose heart is loyal to Him.
II Chronicles 16:9

> God wants to do powerful things through you to prove He exists. You just have to choose to be yielded to Him.

Then the children of Israel who had returned from captivity ate together with all who had separated themselves from filth of the nations in order to seek the Lord.
Ezra 6:21

> We can be set free from bad habits and sin. As the Israelites were freed from bondage, we need to eat (or hang out with) others who refuse to stoop to the culturally accepted sin. Separate yourself and spend time with God so you will be strengthened.

So we fasted and entreated God for this and He answered our prayers.
Ezra 8:23

> Ezra prayed for God's protection rather than rely on help from the king's army. When we trust God, not worldly solutions to our problems, He is faithful.

And between the upper room at the corner, as far as the Sheep Gate, the goldsmiths and the merchants made repairs.
Nehemiah 3:32

(These verses name individuals working side-by-side to rebuild the wall in Jerusalem. Each had a different skill and had to do his best so the wall would be secure). God expects us to do our best each day for His kingdom working together with other Christians for the good of the Gospel. Stay faithful, choose good, do your best.

Remember me, my God for good according to all that I have done...
Nehemiah 5:19

I hope we, too, can say this for using our time, resources, and lives to do good and glorify God while we live.

Do not sorrow for the joy of the Lord is your strength.
Nehemiah 8:10

Even when we face loss or hardship, we can have joy knowing God sees us, and He will give us strength to go on.

So I brought their leaders upon the wall and appointed two large thanksgiving choirs.
Nehemiah 12:31

> This was for a dedication of the wall after its completion. Two things are important here: acknowledging God's help for our accomplishments and singing praises to Him.
>
> As you prepare for graduation think about doing this.

Letters were sent to destroy and kill all Jews, young and old, children and women.
Esther 3:13

> These people did nothing wrong. They were hated for who they were. Prejudice is devilish and illogical. We all need to check that we don't make glib remarks that encourage the attitude of prejudice against anyone.

Who knows whether you have come to the kingdom for such a time as this.
Esther 4:14

> This scripture prompts us to speak out for God and his righteousness even when it is not popular. We are here to stand up and make Him known.

*Mordecai the Jew was second to the king...
seeking good of his people and speaking
peace.*
Esther 10:3

Do you want to be popular? Here's how. Do what's good for others and bring peace, not division, between friends.

*Then the Lord said, "Have you considered
my servant Job?"*
Job 1:8

Now I don't know about you, but I don't want God pointing me out to Satan so he can pick on me. But God did this to Job. Then He explained why. "There's none like him on earth, blameless, upright, fears God, and shuns evil."

God was bragging like a proud father because He knew He could trust Job's faithfulness. Like Job, I hope that God can trust me.

Behold happy is the man whom God corrects.
Job 5:17

Correction is not always pleasant, but when you know it comes from God, you can accept and submit knowing it will be for your growth in Christ and will result in joy.

How can a man be righteous before God?
Job 9:2

> Job asked this knowing man can't measure up to a holy God. But we who have accepted Jesus as our Savior are washed from our sin and can stand before God with no fear but love.

Your hands have made and fashioned me...
Job 10:8

> God took great care to make you special. A big temptation is to try to be something we're not. Thank God for how you are made with your looks, abilities, and sensibilities. God takes pleasure in you, just the way you are.

Though He slay me, yet will I trust Him.
Job 13:15

> You will go through difficulties, sometimes as a result of your own doings, sometimes it's just part of living. But we can trust God to give us strength, and we can trust Him to bring us to victory.

*How many are my iniquities and sins?
Make me know my transgressions and sins.*
Job 13:23

> Job was brave to ask God this. We should too. If you really want to please God, ask Him to show you what He wants to change, then let Him.

For I know that my Redeemer lives...
Job 20:25

> Job knew this without a doubt. Do you know Jesus lives? Ask Him to be real to you. You will be able to say as Job did, "I know that my Redeemer lives!"

I have treasured the words of His mouth more than my necessary food.
Job 23:12

> In the midst of his suffering, Job wanted to hear from God more than eat. How many times a day are we putting something in our mouths? Do we desire to pray or read the Word as often? Let's try.

The fear of the Lord, that is wisdom, to depart from evil is understanding.
Job 28:28

Fearing God means you love Him so much you hate whatever is opposd to Him. Evil is anything that is against the Law and love of God.

My heart is in turmoil, and I cannot rest.
Job 30:27

Job was not denying his physical or emotional suffering. He felt turmoil nothing, made sense, and he ached to see things right again. Even in this, Job wasn't blaming God, merely expressing his true feelings. Don't feel despair when you feel this way. Look to God and wait for Him to bring you peace and hope.

He is not partial to princes, nor does He regard rich more than poor; For they are all the work of His hands.
Job 34:19

We are so saturated in our culture that worships money and success. That is not how God sees value, since He gave some the ability to earn more than others. Don't look down on those who have less. God loves them and trusts you to love and help those you can.

He drew a circular horizon on the face of the waters...
Job 36:10

We don't know who wrote Job or when, but it is thought to be one of the oldest writings. Here God has hidden the fact that the earth is round. It's too bad people didn't read this during the period of exploration when they thought the earth was flat. The Bible tells us the truth about everything. Read it and you will be wise.

Stand still and consider the wondrous works of God.
Job 37:14

Unclutter your mind; end your worry. Stop! Go outside; look up at the sky or down into the garden. Listen to God through nature. Observe His power and care. Bask in His presence.

Look now at the behemoth which I made along with you.
Job 40:15

God is describing a giant creature like a dinosaur. Here is a scripture that disproves evolution. This creature lived the same time as man, Scientists have found fossil footprints of humans along with those of dinosaurs proving they coexisted not lived thousands of years apart. The Bible is the most reliable source we have. Science needs to catch up with what was written by God.

And the Lord restored Job's losses when he prayed.
Job 42:10

Throughout Job's story, his friends were falsely accusing Job of sin to explain God allowing his tragedies. Now, God told Job to pray for them, which helped him to forgive them. When he did, God blessed Job beyond all he had previously. Forgiveness always brings blessings back to us.

Blessed is the man who walks not in the counsel of the ungodly...but delights in the law of the Lord.
Psalm 1:1-2

That word blessed can mean happy. Do you want to be happy? Don't be influenced by ungodly ideas and people. Instead look to God's Word for guidance and information (truth).

Now therefore, be wise, O kings, be instructed, you judges of the earth. Serve the Lord with fear and rejoice with trembling.
Psalm 2:10

This hymn refers to when Jesus will return to judge the earth. He rewards the wise, who no matter how exalted a position, listened to God's Word and served his purposes. They will reverence God, and joy was the result. Let's remember no matter how smart we think we are, God will teach us His way of doing things that brings joy.

But you O Lord, are a shield for me, my glory and the One who lifts my head.
Psalm 3:3

> This is so comforting. God is a shield or protection against the power of darkness, and He will lift our thoughts from despair to hope. Keep your thoughts on His Word.

I will both lie down in peace, and sleep: for You alone, O Lord, make me to dwell in safety.
Psalm 4:8

> If you want a good night's sleep, always talk with God before you lie down. Pour out your concerns and settle any offences. Then, you will have peace. Meditate on this: you will dwell in safety.

For You, O Lord, will bless the righteous with favor, You will surround him with a shield.
Psalm 5:12

> When you surrender your life to Jesus, you are considered righteous before God. If so, this promise is for you. It gives me joy and a feeling of safety.

*O, Lord, do not rebuke me in Your anger,
nor chasten me in Your hot displeasure.
Have mercy on me O Lord, for I am weak.
Psalm 6:1-2*

David was going through a hard time when he wrote
this. He paid consequences for his sin but never lost
favor with God. God will not let you go, but you may
miss out on blessings if you indulge in things that are
harmful. Pray to stay strong in your commitment to
obey God.

*O righteous God, who searches minds and
hearts, bring an end to the wicked and
make the righteous secure.
Psalm 7:9*

God knows what's in our thoughts and what we desire,
so be honest when you talk with God. The second part
is a prayer we can agree with; stop the wicked and keep
us safe. Amen

When I consider the heavens, the work of your finger, the moon and the stars, which You have ordained, what is man the You are mindful of him?
Psalm 8:3-4

> This reminds us how vast is God's creation. He made everything and set it all in motion, and yet little you are on His mind. He thinks about you and wants only good in your life.

I will praise You, O Lord, with my whole heart; I will tell of all Your marvelous works.
Psalm 9:1

> Take time each night to thank God for something He did for you that day. That is praise and it will help you develop your spiritual muscle. Share it and it will encourage others in their faith.

Why do you stand afar off, O Lord?
Psalm 10:1

> Sometimes we wonder why God doesn't help us against injustice like this writer. God seems far away. But as we finish this Psalm, the writer assures us that God sees all and will defend the helpless in the end. Persevere in hardship. There will be victory with God on your side.

The Lord tests the righteous, but the wicked and the ones who love violence His soul hates.
Psalm 11:5

Troubles come. Sometimes it is the Lord testing us to stand on His Word and allow the Holy Spirit to strengthen us. But the wicked are dealt with to correct. God is just.

May the Lord cut off all flattering lips and the tongue that speaks proud things,
Psalm 12:3

Wow! This sound serious. Flattery is an insincere compliment usually for personal gain. God doesn't like it. We (especially women) can be deceived by it. Prideful words or boasting is just as dishonest. Watch out! You don't want your lips cut off, nor do you want to follow after a liar.

I will sing to the Lord because He has treated me generously.
Psalm 13:6

David started this Psalm in deep despair. It is a cry for victory over his enemy. But David confessed his trust in God and even before he had victory, David started praising and singing to God with gratefulness.

The fool has said in his heart, "There is no God."
Psalm 14:1

There you have it. People who don't want to acknowledge truth and the obvious are corrupt or just fools.

Who may dwell in Your sanctuary?... who lends money without interest and does not accept a bribe against the innocent.
Psalm 15:1-5

God is against making a profit on loans to the needy or fellow believers. It was alright to charge foreigners. The point is don't let money be your driving force. Be generous and give freely to those who need help.

You will show me the path of life; in your presence is fulness of joy. At your right hand are pleasures forever more.
Psalm 16:11

> This sounds good to me. Seek God's presence and you will have joy and pleasure.

You have visited me in the night.
Psalm 17:3

> God never sleeps, and He will speak to you even in your dreams. I have prayed for direction, and God gave me a vivid dream of what I had to do. Sometimes, nighttime is the only time we are quiet enough to listen to God.

Uphold my steps in your paths that my footsteps may not slip.
Psalm 17:5

> David prayed this. I suggest you do too, every morning before your feet hit the ground.

I shall be satisfied when I awake in your likeness.
Psalm 17:15

This is the goal of a Christian; to be transformed from the inside by the Holy Spirit into the character of our Lord Jesus Christ. It takes humility and yielding our wills for His. But you will be amazed at how much better you will look. I hope I will awake in His likeness.

I will love you, O Lord, my strength.
Psalm 18:1

When you learn to depend on God, He will not disappoint. When you are weak, He is strong. Ask for help (without me you can do nothing. John 15:5) and don't forget to say you love Him.

He drew me out of the waters, He delivered me from my enemy.
Psalm 18:16,19

Sometimes we find ourselves drowning or overcome with temptation and sin. That is the devil trying to destroy you. But God will lift you out of that. Verse 19… "He delivered me because He delighted in me." God delights in you. I do too.

The heavens declare the glory of God and the sky proclaims the work of His hand. Day after day they pour out speech; night after night they communicate knowledge.
Psalm 19:1

These verses tell us that all men should know there is a God. The wonders of the sky and beauty of the earth are shouting, "He Is Here!" There is no excuse to deny God.

Let the words of my mouth and the meditation of my heart be acceptable in your sight.
Psalm 19:14

Whether you acknowledge it or not, God hears your every word and knows your every thought. We should delight in His company and make sure he enjoys ours.

May the Lord answer you in the day of trouble. May the name of the God of Jacob defend you.
Psalm 20:1

When frustrations and situations come up, don't forget to call on Jesus for help to guide and defend you. All you have to say is, "Jesus, help!" Demons must flee at His name and like a dad, He wants to help you and see you succeed.

Be exalted, O Lord, in Your own strength! We will sing and praise your power.
Psalm 21:13

David was praising God for answered prayer. Think over all the things you prayed for and thank God for His power to answer them.

I will declare Your name to my brethren; in the midst of the assembly, I will praise You.
Psalm 22:22

This is a desire I pray for you; to tell others about our Savior, Jesus Christ and never to be ashamed to praise Him before others.

This Psalm contains prophecy of all Jesus would suffer on the cross. We should be willing to speak up for Him.

He makes me lie down in green pastures;
He leads me beside still waters.
Psalm 23:2

> Think of Jesus as your Shepherd. Sometimes you don't know what is best for you, but the Good Shepherd does. When He tells you to stop and rest, it's in a good place. Trust Him and wait. When He leads you to drink it is good safe water, not rushing tide. Listen to His voice.

The earth is the Lord's and all its fullness;
the world and those who dwell therein.
Psalm 24:1

> I like this. It gives me a sense of belonging. I'm glad I belong to God and live in His world.

Make Your ways known to me, Lord. Teach me your paths, Guide me in Your truth and teach me for You are the God of my salvation.
Psalm 25:4-5

I have trusted in the Lord. I shall not slip.
Psalm 26:1

> Set your eyes on God and trust in His guidance by His Spirit and through His word. You will not fail or fall.

One thing I have desired of the Lord, that I will seek: that I may dwell in the house of the Lord all the days of my life.
Psalm 27:4

> We know that if we are believers, we will dwell with God in heavenly places, but you can behold the beauty of the Lord now. Take time to seek Him through prayer and Bible reading. You will experience His love and presence.

The Lord is my strength and my shield; my heart trusted in Him, and I am helped.
Psalm 28:7

> There are times when we are weary and weak. Call on God for His strength. When we ask and trust God, He will come through. It is exhilarating to see the power of God work in us ("When I am weak, then I am strong." II Corinthians 12:10)

The voice of the Lord is over the waters; the God of glory thunders.
Psalm 29:3

I have always loved the sound of powerful waves crashing, and the louder the thunder the better. I am in awe of these magnificent displays of God's power and ability to get my attention.

Weeping may endure for a night, but joy comes in the morning.
Psalm 30:5

We will have disappointments, failures, heartache, and discipline. These hurt, but don't despair. Wait! Circumstances change. Hope will be rewarded. Joy will return. Verse 11 says, "You have turned my mourning into dancing."

But as for me, I trust in you, O Lord. I say, "You are my God."
Psalm 31:14

Never be ashamed to tell people about the hope that is in you. You need not be afraid to stand against the majority who don't have faith in Christ. Stand up and profess Him as Savior and Lord, He will stand up for you.

*How joyful is the one whose transgression
is forgiven, whose sin is covered.*
Psalm 32:1

How do you know your sin is forgiven? Verse 5 says,
"I will confess my sin to the Lord, and You took away
the guilt of my sin."

The earth is filled with the goodness of the Lord.
Psalm 33:5

TV, podcasts, movies, can be depressing. Let's not
focus on that. Go outside. Lift your head and look
around at our beautiful surroundings. "The earth is of
the goodness of God."

Blessed is the nation whose God is the Lord.
Psalm 33:12

This is a wonderful promise and America was founded
on Judeo-Christian values by men who acknowledged
and worshipped God. Pray for a leader who will be a
faithful Christian so our country will continue to be
blessed.

No king is saved by the multitude of an army; a mighty man is not delivered by great strength.
Psalm 33:16

This is a reminder that our victories come from God. Prepare the best you can, but ask God for the victory. He has the power.

I will bless the Lord at all times; His praise shall continually be in my mouth.
Psalm 34:1

This is how to have joy. Give God praise and gratitude all day long. Look for all the little things that go right and say, "Thanks to God!"

Taste and see that the Lord is good; blessed is the man who takes refuge in Him.
Psalm 34:8

To taste something, you must take it in. Being a Christian is more than knowing about Jesus You must take in every word and promise, and let it become a part of your life.

Keep your tongue from evil and your lips
from speaking deceit. Depart from evil and
do good; seek peace and pursue it.
Psalm 34:13-14

> This is your daily list. Simply don't speak badly, stay
> away from evil, but on the positive side, do good, and
> seek peace with everyone.

I will give you thanks in the great assembly;
I will praise you among many people.
Psalm 35:18

> When God answers prayer, share it with someone.
> This will build their faith and yours. It will please God.

How precious is Your lovingkindness, O,
God! Therefore, the children of men put
their trust under the shadow of Your wings.
Psalm 36:7

> I love this description of lovingkindness. God is
> nurturing and protecting us as a mother bird cares for
> her young. I just want to cuddle up to God.

They are filled from the abundance of your house; You let them drink from Your refreshing stream.
Psalm 36:8

A refreshing drink is a good way to describe our need for God. This would, with our stresses, create a thirst for peace and safety. When we feel empty, draw close to God. (Talk to Him).

Trust in the Lord and do good.
Psalm 37:3

I make this my plan every day. Look for somewhere you can give, encourage, or share each day and trust God to bless and guide you.

Delight yourself in the Lord and He will give you the desires of your heart. Commit your way to the Lord; trust Him and He will do this.
Psalm 37:4-5

Here is a promise. If we look solely to God and commit all we do to Him, He will bring forth fulfillment. When God gives you the desires of your heart, it means He puts godly desires in your heart and will bring completion and joy into your heart.

The steps of a good man are ordered by the Lord, and He delights in his way. Though he falls, he shall not be utterly cast down; For the Lord upholds him with His hand.
Psalm 37:23-24

Ask God each morning to order your steps (plan your day). Do what He prompts, and God takes pleasure in you. You may fail at times, but God has you in His hand and will help you along the way. Don't be discouraged. God's got you covered.

Depart from evil and do good...
Psalm 37:27

Simple. Anything contrary to God's Word is evil. Seek to do good; the promise is His favor and protection.

The wicked watches the righteous and seeks to slay him.
Psalm 37:32

If you love Jesus and speak up for Him, you will have opposition. Be prepared and don't be discouraged. Read this verse in Psalm 37:40. "The Lord shall help you and deliver you from the wicked...because you trust Him." There is victory over your enemies.

For I will declare my iniquity; I will be in anguish over my sin.
Psalm 38:18

> I think this reveals if you are Spirit-filled. We will sometimes sin, but if you love Jesus, you will regret it and want to confess it and be renewed. I hope we all feel anguish when we sin.

Lord, make me to know my end, and what is the measure of my days, that I may know how frail I am.
Psalm 39:4

> This would be nice if we knew exactly how many days we have, but we don't. We need to fill everyday with actions that please God. Use your time wisely and depend on God completely.

I waited patiently for the Lord; and He inclined to me and heard my cry.
Psalm 40:1

> Waiting patiently isn't easy for us, but we are to presevere in prayer. I think God waits to give us an answer because He loves to hear from us. Talk with Him often and know He hears you.

He brought me up from a desolate pit, out of the miry clay and set my feet on a rock, making my steps secure.
Psalm 40:2-3

When we become accustomed to sin, we are sliding into a mirky pit. You can't stop without God's power. When you give Him permission, God will lift you out. That rock is Jesus. Depend on Him. Stand on His word.

I delight to do your will, O My God. Your law is in my heart.
Psalm 40:8

After you've made enough mistakes and paid the consequences, you are ready to do things God's way. We know His will by reading the Bible, praying, and then asking Him to lead. Do you think you will miss out on anything?

As the deer pants for the water brooks, pants my soul for You, O God.
Psalm 41:1

I love this image. We should be as thirsty deer running to refreshing water. Only God can provide that satisfaction and needed nourishment to our tired hungry souls. Quit striving for things and recognition. Only God can satisfy you completely.

Then I will go to the alter of God, to God my exceeding joy; and on harp I will praise You O God, my God.
Psalm 43:4

David wrote this when he was feeling low and defeated. He was crying out to God. He realized there is hope in God. He took his focus off his problem, looked to God, and praised God for who He is… the help of our countenance.

Through You we will push down our enemies.
Psalm 44:5

> Some days we feel that opposition of the devil to keep us from overcoming temptation, from getting our study and work done, and destroying relationships. That's when we need to send a prayer that God will stop the devil's attacks and give us victory by the Holy Spirit. Try tapping into His power.

I will make Your name to be remembered in
all generations...
Psalm 45:17

> When we recognize how much God has done for us, we want to tell others about Him. Open your heart and eyes each day to what He does for you and share it with each other.

God is our refuge and strength, a very present help in trouble. Therefore, we will not fear.
Psalm 46:1-2

We hear bad news and doom around the world, but as Christians we should not despair. First of all, God is our refuge or protection. Nothing touches you that God cannot control. When we are weak, He is stronger. Don't fear, but put your trust in God's ability to keep you.

O clap your hands all you peoples! Shout to God with a voice of triumph! For the Lord Most High is awesome.
Psalm 47:1-2

I like to worship God with melodious hymns and gentle words, but God likes the loud clapping and shouting praises as our contemporary worship today. So, I must join in.

Great is the Lord and worthy of Praise in the city of Our God (Jerusalem) His holy mountain.
Psalm 48:1

> Two things here: God is worthy because there is nothing you are or have that did not come from Him; Jerusalem is important because the temple was there, and it was the center of God's presence. In the last day, believers will gather there.

Those who trust in their wealth and boast of their riches, none of them can redeem his brother, nor give to God a ransom for him.
Psalm 49:6-7

> No matter how rich you are, you can't buy salvation. Riches will be left behind at death, but salvation continues for eternity.

Call upon Me in the day of trouble; I will deliver you, and you shall glorify Me.
Psalm 50:15

> We have trouble going through this life. God allows it so we will learn to ask Him for help. He wants us to experience His power and care. Then, we can tell others about His reality.

Create in me a clean heart, O God, and renew a right spirit within me.
Psalm 51:10

> When we sin (and we will), God wants us to come as David with grief and sorrow. True repentance means not to engage in it again. We are cleansed by the blood of Jesus, but we, too should ask God to infill us with His Holy Spirit so our desires can be changed by His presence. That is how we live in Christ.

The sacrifices of God are a broken spirit, a broken and contrite heart.
Psalm 51:17

> There is nothing we can do to make amends for our sin. Jesus, a sacrifice for us, paid our debt. But a true child of God will grieve over sin because we hurt the God who loves us.

I am like a green olive tree in the house of God.
Psalm 52:8

> This Psalm compared those who disobey God with those who heed His word. Those who love evil more than good will be uprooted and destroyed. I pray you will obey and love God and flourish as a green olive tree.

The fool has said in his heart, "There is no God."
Psalm 53:1

> That says it all about those who think they don't need God. They let pride keep them from acknowledging the Truth.

Behold, God is my helper; The Lord is with those who uphold my life.
Psalm 54:4

> David was on the run, and he knew God would be there to defend him. God is for us, even when our enemy (Satan) is close on our tail. Call out like David. Watch what God will do.

Give ear to my prayer, O God, and do not hide Yourself from my supplication.
Psalm 55:1

> David was feeling distraught and alone. He cried to God to hear him. Isaiah 65:24 tells us that God hears us before we can speak and answers us while we are still speaking. You are not alone, and God wants to help.

You number my wandering; put my tears into Your bottle.
Psalm 56:8

> God cares about your struggles and sorrows. He sees you. He saves your tears. Nothing we go through in this life is unseen or wasted by God.

Be merciful to me, O God, be merciful to me!
Psalm 57:1

> David was running for his life. He knew he had offended God, but he asked for mercy (not getting what you deserve) and protection. Verse 1b says, "And in the shadow of your wings I will make refuge."
>
> I love that picture of being close to God sheltered by His strength and care.

Do you indeed speak righteousness, you silent ones? Do you judge uprightly, you sons of men? No, in your heart you work wickedness.
Psalm 58:1-2

This is harsh news to share with you, but just as David saw then, we see now our judges are not always just. We are still to obey our laws and wait on God for real justice. Verse 11 says, "Surely there is a reward for the righteous; Surely God judges the earth."

Our hope is in God. Walk circumspectly (carefully).

Deliver me from my enemies, O God, protect me from those who rise up against me.
Psalm 59:1

We too, have an enemy who won't give up. John 10:10 says, "The thief comes to steal, kill, and destroy." This is Satan, and he will use devices to steal your blessings, and successes, kill your sense of morality and self-worth, and destroy your life. Pray you recognize his tactics and run to God for protection.

Give us help in trouble, for the help of man
is useless. Through God we will do valiantly,
for it is He who treads down our enemies.
Psalm 60:11-12

> When we are up against the devil, our first instinct
> should be to call upon God. He has the power and
> wisdom to bring victory in our lives. We would save a
> lot of time if we did.

From the ends of the earth I call you. I
call as my heart grows faint; lead me to the
rock that is higher than I.
Psalm 61:2

> There are so many times we humans feel weak and at
> the end of our efforts. It could be in study, overcoming
> temptation, or work. But God has strength like a rock,
> and as believers He wants to give us strength to do
> over and beyond what we alone are able. Call on Him;
> He is waiting.

My soul waits silently for God alone, for my expectation is from Him.
Psalm 62:5

Waiting for God is not always easy. We want our things and our own way, now. But God wants your devotion and attention. When you turn your desire to Him, it is funny how all your wants and needs are met. Try it. Give Him your heart and take time to tell Him.

If riches increase, do not set your heart on them.
Psalm 62:10

There is no arguing that it is better to have money than not. You can do much good for others. Buy yourself nice things and be comfortable. But don't make these things your god. Everything comes from God. Show appreciation by thanking Him and use your resources wisely.

Because Your lovingkindness is better than life, my lips shall praise You.
Psalm 63:3

Lovingkindness refers to God's mercy and faithful love. It never ceases. Think of times you have experienced His mercy and love and praise or thank Him.

When I think of You as I lie on my bed, I meditate on You during the night watches because You are my helper.
Psalm 63:6

Jesus should be the first one you think about in the morning and the last one you think on and talk to at night. Meditate means to think about. As you lie in bed, think of all He's done for you that day and praise Him for keeping you "in the shadow of His wing." Psalm 63:7

Hide me from the secret plots of the wicked, from the rebellion of workers of iniquity.
Psalm 64:2

I pray this daily, that God will hide us from evil people and that we do not becomes victims of evil plots. We must take steps to stay on the path God has for us. Stay away from the ungodly and keep your heart fixed on doing good not evil.

How happy is the one You choose and bring near to live in Your courts.
Psalm 65:4

> We are chosen by God to live close to Him in peace and be blessed. Stay there. Don't look elsewhere for contentment. It only exists in God's presence.

Those who live far away are awed by Your signs; You make east and west shout for joy.
Psalm 65:8

> Nature is beyond our description, whether in words or by paintbrush. I like this reference of nature shouting for joy. Take time to look at the sky, stars, moon, and mountains. Shout for joy at God's creation.

If I regard iniquity in my heart, the Lord will not hear. But certainly, God has heard me.
Psalm 66:18-19

> When we pray, we should include honest confession of any offenses. Our sin often keeps God from answering our prayers.
>
> 1 John 1:9 says, "If we confess our sins, He is faithful and just to forgive our sins."

God be merciful to us and bless us, and cause Your face to shine upon us, that Your way maybe known on earth.
Psalm 67:1-2

> I want God's face to shine on me. We should be like the moon which reflects the sun's light. As we experience God's love, we should reflect it to those around us.

A father to the fatherless, a defender of widows, is God in His habitation.
Psalm 68:5

> This scripture was a comfort to me raising Winnie alone. This confirms God would be her father, and He would defend me from the fiery darts of Satan. And you know, He did all that and more.

God sets the lonely in families. He leads forth the prisoners with singing but the rebellious live in a sun scorched land.
Psalm 68:6

What a contrast. Those who draw near to God eat with, love, and support people who comfort and are trustworthy. Even when circumstances are tough, we can have joy and songs in our hearts knowing God will help us. But those who shun God are wanting and empty. Stay in His Word, pray daily, and don't lose faith.

The God of Israel is He who gives strength and power to His people.
Psalm 68:35

This is repeated often. God wants to empower you. You don't have to do anything on your own. Ask Him for strength to help you in your studies, work, and play.

Hear me, O Lord, for Your lovingkindness is good; Turn to me according to the multitude of Your tender. Mercies. Do not hide Your face from Your servant, for I am in trouble.
Psalm 69:16-17

> God is the best one to run to when you are in trouble. Not only does He love you without measure, but He can change the circumstances that beat you down. Life can be hard, but God will lift you up.

Let those who seek You rejoice.
Psalm 70:4

> David said this as he was crying out to God to deliver them from his enemies. David knew that God would defend him. We should rejoice too. God will not let us down when we cry for help.

In You, O Lord I put my trust; Let me never be put to shame.
Psalm 71:1

> Stand up for God. Speak out His Word. You will not be shamed. People may disagree or snicker, but God will bring reward and honor to you. I would rather have God's favor than the approval of man.

*For He will deliver the needy when he cries,
the poor also, and him who has no helper.
Psalm 72:12*

God has great compassion on the poor and lonely and so should we who have been given so much. Look out for those you can help. God wants to use you as His hands and heart.

*Behold, these are the ungodly, who are at ease; They increase in riches. Surely, I have cleansed my heart in vain.
Psalm 73:12-13*

Often, we see those who cheat and act wickedly get ahead or prosper. But get a heavenly perspective. God will eventually deal with them. Stay strong in the Lord, and don't compromise your values. You will have prosperity according to God's reward system.

*Whom have I in heaven but You? And earth has nothing I desire besides you.
Psalm 73:25*

It is so freeing to get to the point that all you want is to know the Lord, do His will, and trust Him for everything you need. Start today. Practice acknowledging His many blessings.

It is good for me to draw near to God; I have put my trust in the Lord God, that I may declare all Your works.
Psalm 73:28

Are you desiring companionship or strength to get things done? Do you need help? Draw near to God. Trust Him to meet all your needs. I do, and He has not failed me yet.

Rise up, O God, and defend your cause; remember how fools mock you all day long.
Psalm 74:22

God is so patient with humans. Remember, "He's not wanting any should perish but all to come to repentance." Now if a fool mocks, should we bristle up and take offense? No, he is a fool, and all he says is a lie. Brush it off. Look to the source.

*Exaltation comes neither from the east not
from the west nor from the south, but God
is the Judge: He puts down one and exalts
another.*
Psalm 75:6-7

> Don't be discouraged if you see others get fame or
> recognition when you have worked harder. God
> will exalt you in His time. Be humble. Be honest. Be
> steadfast and give thanks.

*Make vows to the Lord your God and pay
them.*
Psalm 76:11

> God takes seriously the vows we make to Him. Let
> your words be sincere and honest. Remember Proverbs
> 6:19. God hates a false witness who speaks lies.

*I will remember the works of the Lord;
Surely, I will remember Your wonders of old.*
Psalm 77:11

> Sometimes we focus on our circumstances and difficulties.
> This leads to despair. Instead, think on how much God
> has brought you through. Read God's Word and study
> His faithfulness to those He loves. (You are one.)

We will not hide from their children; we will tell the next generation the praiseworthy deeds of the Lord.
Psalm 78:4

It is up to parents and grandparents to tell you about Jesus and the Truth that is in the Bible. You will hear so much from others that is not truth, but if you are wise, you come to this conclusion: you can put your trust in Jesus and believe His Word.

He rained down manna for the people to eat. He gave them bread from heaven.
Psalms 78:24

Even today, God wants to supply the very best for you. Don't be like the Israelites and complain that you want your way. God may give it to you as He did the Israelites. It ended in disaster. Praise and thank Him and ask that you may be willing to follow Him.

We, Your people and sheep of Your pastures will give You thanks for ever.
Psalm 79:13

I love this image that we are God's sheep being watched over and cared for. Take time to give Him thanks and praise. We are in His loving hands.

Revive us. We will call upon Your name. Restore us YAHWEH, cause Your face to shine upon us, and we will be saved.
Psalm 80:18

The psalmist is calling upon God. He repents and asks for restoration. We too, will make mistakes and feel far from God. Pray God revives your heart (makes it new) and ask for favor. You will be restored and feel like new.

Oh, that Israel would walk in My ways!...
Psalm 81:13

I would have feed them with the finest of wheat as honey out of the rock.
Psalm 81:16

I wonder how much I missed by not walking with the Lord. Let's not miss out anymore but seek daily to walk according to God's precepts. Ask to have Him order your steps daily.

Defend the poor and the fatherless; do justice to the afflicted and needy.
Psalm 82:3

> We are told to take care of and stand up for those who have no power to care for themselves. We are so privileged. Let's be aware when God is asking us to give, share, and speak up for those who struggle.

Don't keep silent, O God! Do not hold your peace and do not be still, O God!
Psalm 83:1

> The psalmist is begging God to intervene as the enemies were destroying them. Sometimes we must hold on in hard times. Eventually God will be victorious over our enemies. We need to keep our faith in Him. Pray for the people of Ukraine not to lose heart.

Blessed are those whose strength is in You, who have set their hearts on pilgrimage as they pass through the Valley of Baca, they make it a place of springs...
Psalm 84:5-6

When we are determined to walk with God, we are on a journey that can be a difficult dry valley. Many of your friends will leave you or make fun of you because you have higher standards than you see portrayed in movies etc. But let it be a place of refreshment as you call on God for His presence and Spirit to take you through this time of testing.

A day in your court is better than a thousand, I would rather be a doorkeeper in the house of God than dwell in the tents of wickedness.
Psalm 84:10

Remember it is better to do the right thing than take deceptive steps to get ahead. A little with God is a lot.

For God is a sun and shield; the Lord bestows favor and honor; no good thing does He withhold from those whose walk is blameless.
Psalm 84:11

> Picture this: God gives us light or direction, protects us, gives us favoritism and honor. You won't miss out on any good thing He has, but all you need to do is live according to His precepts. Study His Word so you know which way to take.

The Lord shall give that which is good...
Psalm 85:12

> God will always give us good things. "Every good and perfect gift is from God." James 1:17 Take time to thank Him.

Give ear, O Lord to my prayers attend to the voice of my supplications.
Psalm 86:6

Do you think God listens to you when you call to Him, when you're hurting, or need help? Or do you think He brushes you off and thinks, "Later?" I hope you sincerely know that you are so important to God that He is always listening for your voice and wanting to help you. Stop and tell Him you love Him.

Glorious things are spoken of you, O city of God!
Psalm 87:3

This is referring to Jerusalem, and it is a prophecy that Christ will be born there. Old Testament prophecies completed are proof that the Bible was written by the Holy Spirit and we, too, can be sure God will keep His promises to us.

But to you, I cried out, O Lord, and in the morning my prayer comes before You.
Psalm 88:13

It is paramount to ask God for His protection form evil, to guide our steps, and to fill us with the Holy Spirit every morning. Don't get out of bed without giving this short prayer. It will make a difference.

I will sing of the mercies of the Lord forever.
Psalm 89:1

Mercy is not getting what you deserve because our God is forgiving and wants to bless us. Think of the times you were spared rebuke or consequences when you were in the wrong. Then sing out a praise to the Almighty God who loves you.

Lord, you have been our dwelling place in all generations.
Psalm 90:1

Think about this: a dwelling place is where you go at the end of the day to rest, refresh, and find safety and comfort. Make God's presence be your dwelling place. There's no better place to be.

Teach us to number our days carefully so that we may develop wisdom.
Psalm 90:12

It's ok to have fun activities, but use your time wisely. Don't waste time on activities that lead you away from God. Let your efforts be in pursuit of knowing God and doing His will. Then you will acquire wisdom. That is a good use of time.

Let the favor of the Lord rest upon us; establish the work of our hands.
Psalm 90:17

God has always provided work for me. Sometimes it was hard, but God showed me favor with strength and good health.

For He shall give His angels charge over you, to keep you in all your ways.
Psalm 91:11

This should make us feel safe, knowing God sends angelic beings to protect us. I can think of times when I know angels have intervened on my behalf.

*Because he has set his love upon Me,
therefore, I will deliver him.*
Psalm 91:14

> How do we get free of those habits that keep us in
> bondage (temper, smoking, vaping, overeating,
> drinking,)? Get your focus on God (think on Him).
> What you think about affects what you do. God will
> set you free from bad habits if you let Him.

*It is good to give thanks to the Lord, and
sing praises to Your name, O Most High.*
Psalm 92:1

> If the Bible says it is good to do something, why
> wouldn't you do it? Give thanks and praise to God
> throughout your day. It will give you joy and an
> awareness of His presence.

*The Lord on high is mightier than the
noise of many waters...*
Psalm 93:4

> I love going down to the harbor and listening to the
> waves crash on the rocks. It exemplifies the power of
> the sea but also the power of the One who created it.
> Remind yourself to go to Him when you feel powerless.
> Isaiah 40:29 says, "He gives strength to the weary."

Who will rise up against evil doers? Who will stand for Me against worker of iniquity?
Psalm 94:11

This is a question for all of us and should lead us to action. We live in a time when evil is acceptable, and few speak up to say this behavior is wrong. But God is asking us to speak up that His Word is truth and living contrary to it is evil. Study His word so you can speak with confidence that what God has given is right.

Oh come, let us worship and bow down; let us kneel before the Lord our Maker. For He is our God, and we are the people of His pasture, and the sheep of His hand.
Psalm 95:6-7

We kneel before God in gratitude and awe because the One who created all things holds you in His hand to love and protect. Try kneeling before Him.

Today if you hear His voice; do not harden your hearts as in...
Psalm 95:7,8

So I swore in my wrath, "They shall not enter My rest."
Psalm 95:11

If you know God is speaking to you about your commitment, a bad habit, or your disobedience, don't harden your heart toward God on your way. As with those who ignored God at Meribah, you will reap misery. Why not listen, obey, and receive His blessings?

Sing to the Lord, bless His name: proclaim the good news of His salvation from day to day.
Psalm 96:2

Sing to God, even if you don't like your voice. (God likes it.) Use His name in love (not casually). Tell others about Jesus' sacrifice for sin and love for all sinners.

The Lord reigns...He shall judge the earth righteously.
Psalm 96:10

> God is the ultimate judge, and He is righteous and fair. There is much in our world that is not just. "All have sinned," but if you turn from sin and follow Jesus, you will be judged as innocent. That is God's justice. Jesus took your judgement on the cross.

You who love the Lord, hate evil. He preserves the souls of His saints. He delivers them out of the hand of the wicked.
Psalm 97:10

> Here is a gauge to see how much you love God. Do you like to watch tv or movies that treat sin like an acceptable activity? You should recognize and hate anything contrary to God's precepts. He will keep you from evil, but you must walk away...then vs. 11 Light is sown for the upright in heart.

Rejoice in the Lord, you righteous, and give thanks at the remembrance of His holy name.
Psalm 97:12

There are so many people plagued with anxiety and depression. I think, this verse is a prescription from God. RX: Give thanks in all things; Remember God is holy; Get your mind on Him, not evil. Rejoice! You are righteous, saved, loved, and cared for by a Holy powerful God.

Now take this medicine!

Let the seas roar, and all its fullness, the world and those who dwell in it. Let the rivers clap their hands; Let the hills be joyful together before the Lord, for He is coming to judge the earth with righteousness.
Psalm 98:8-9

I love the use of poetic devices that humanize nature. We do not worship nature but the God who made it to delight our senses. In this passage, we should rejoice like nature at the return of Jesus. It will be good. We will see evil dealt with. We who love Him will be seen as righteous because Jesus paid the price for our sin. That is something to rejoice about; so, roar, clap your hands, and be joyful.

Exalt the Lord our God and worship at his footstool—He is holy.
Psalm 99:5

> The word holy is difficult to define: pure, powerful, love. I think, until you have felt God's presence, you can't understand it. James 4:8 says, "Draw near to God and He will draw near to you."
>
> Pray (on your knees) and ask God to reveal His holiness to you.

Serve the Lord with gladness...It is He who made us, and not we ourselves.
Psalm 100:2-3

> Every day God wants to use us for His purposes: to help someone, to show love, encouragement, or share our faith. He made us for this. Success is just a by-product of a job well done.

I will behave wisely in a perfect way.
Psalm 101:2,3,4,5

> If you're wise, your heart will be for the things of God, and you "will not set wicked things before your eyes: show wickedness, slander anyone, be haughty or prideful."
>
> Ask the Holy Spirit to show you anything you need to change. Behave wisely.

My days are like a shadow that lengthens, and I wither away like grass. But you, O Lord, shall endure forever...
Psalm 102:11-12

I love this image of life as a shadow. My shadow is getting longer as a day the shadows lengthen before the sun sets. Then life is over. It is sad when loved ones pass away, but God will never leave us. He is there forever. Include Him in your life each day.

Bless the Lord O my soul; and all that is within me bless His holy name!
Psalm 103:1-3

(Why should we be so grateful and joyful? Read on.) Bless the Lord, O my soul and forget not His benefits.

(What are the benefits of knowing Jesus? Read on.)

Who forgives your iniquities (sin), who heals all our diseases?

It is no small thing to cleanse us from sin, but God does not remember them or hold past mistakes against you. The last part is important. He heals all our diseases. We should not accept illness, mental or physical, so readily. God heals you! Pray in faith. Don't allow the devil to slow you down.

Who redeems your life from destruction, who crowns you with lovingkindness and tender mercies, who satisfies your mouth with good things so your youth is renewed like an eagle's.
Psalm 103:4-5

> This is a continuance of the list from verse 3 on why we should rejoice and praise God. This list shows how personal God is. He knows what our hearts crave and wants to fulfill us. Sometimes we look to people for what only God can give freely.

As far as the east if from the west, so far has He removed our transgressions from us.
Psalm 103:12

> Sometimes the hardest thing to do is to forgive yourself for your sin. The devil will keep tormenting us with memories. But God's forgiveness is forever. I like the visual of how far east is from west. They never meet. "You are a new creature. Old things are passed away." II Corinthians 5:17

O Lord my God, You are very great; You are clothed with honor and majesty.
Psalm 104:5

Please take time to read this whole Psalm. It beautifully describes God creating the heavens, the earth, and sky, down to little living creatures. We need to remind ourselves how powerful God is and mindful of all creation even you.

He appointed the moon for seasons; the sun knows it's going down.
Psalm 104:19

Look at the beautiful moon or sunset. You can rely on each day that they will be there and be awesome. God created them to show us His presence is constant; His magnificent power dependable; and His blessings beyond our imagination. (He is able to give exceedingly, abundantly above all you ask or think. Ephesians 3:20)

O Lord, how manifest are your works! In wisdom you made them all. The great wide sea... There is that Leviathan which You made to play there.
Psalm 104:24-26

> Don't think we discovered everything. God has so many surprises. And here it is…Lochness (Leviathan). Maybe it still exists. All is for our delight. Don't limit what He can do.

Oh, give thanks to the Lord! Call upon His name; make known His deeds among the peoples!
Psalm 105:1

> Here is a list for today: thank God, ask for God's help for everything, tell others what He has done in your life.

He permitted no one to do them wrong; Yes, He rebuked kings for their sakes, saying, "Do not touch my anointed and do my prophets no harm."
Psalm 105:14-15

I have always felt a sense of protection from God when I know I am walking on the path He has given me. It keeps me from wandering off, because I have done that, and I won't do that again. You are God's property. He watches over you.

And He gave them their request but sent leanness to their soul.
Psalm 106:15

This is taken from one of the saddest accounts. The Israelites instead of thanking God for setting them free from slavery (as we are set free from sin), complained at God's perfect provision and begged to meet their needs in their way. This was disastrous. We too should learn to follow God's leading to bring us into success and not rely on our own tactics.

They made a calf in Horeb and worshiped the molded image. Thus, they changed their glory into the image of an ox that eats grass.
Psalm 106:19-20

The people had seen the power and provision a holy God provided but turned to worship a man-made image of an ox. We need to be on guard that there is nothing we worship or put before our love of God. Where do you draw the line as to following your desires (activities, friends, course jesting, immoral movies) or obeying God?

Then they cried out to the Lord in their trouble, and He delivered them out of their distresses. And He led them forth by the right way.
Psalm 107:6-7

If you are experiencing trouble and distress perhaps you aren't going the right way. Pray before you do anything and then listen to where and what God tells you to do. Then do it!

Give us help from trouble, for the help of man is useless. Through God we will do valiantly, for it is He who shall tread down our enemies.
Psalm 108:12-13

We can get help from friends when in need, but only God can defeat our real enemy, Satan. The devil tries to defeat, steal, and discourage us at every turn. Don't listen to him. Instead, call upon Jesus for victory over the lies of the enemy. Build yourself up with God's promises to overcome.

Help me, Lord my God! Oh, save me according to Your mercy, that they may know that this is Your hand.
Psalm 109:26-27

This is a bitter psalm. David is pleading with God for victory over his enemy. Give God credit for your successes.

The Lord is at Your right hand; He shall execute kings in the day of wrath.
Psalm 110:5

This psalm makes reference to when Jesus shall return to judge the earth. Our God reigns and we will witness evil doers brought to punishment. Don't be discouraged when you see bad people prosper. It will not be for long. Our God Reigns!

The fear of the Lord is the beginning of wisdom; a good understanding to all those who do His commandments.
Psalm 111:10

These words are repeated many times, "fear of the Lord is the beginning of wisdom." Fear means reverence and respect. If we reverence God, we will obey. That is wisdom. Take time to reflect if you are obeying God.

Blessed is the man who fears the Lord, who delights in His commandments.
Psalm 112:1

Some people think of God's commandments as restraints. But this verse is saying that by reverence to God and acknowledging His commands brings joy. God's rules are boundaries to keep you safe and headed for blessings.

From the rising of the sun to it's going down the Lord's name is to be praised.
Psalm 113:3

We are to praise and thank God all day long. This Psalm goes on to tell why; The Lord is above all others, He humbles Himself to come to Earth, He exalts the poor, helps the needy, gives childless women families. What are you thankful for? Praise Him throughout this day!

Tremble, O earth, at the presence of the Lord...Who turned the rock into a pool of water, the flint into a fountain of water.
Psalm 114:7-8

This isn't just fake imagery. God has done these things, and He is not done. When facing impossible situations, run to Him. God still does miracles big and small.

May you be blessed by the Lord, who made heaven and earth.
Psalm 115:15

> If we believe this, God is pleased and will shower you with peace and love.

Precious in the sight of the Lord is the death of His saints.
Psalm 116:15

> All who believe in Jesus are saints. Now, we think of death as sad, but God sees it as precious because you are leaving this world, and you enter into the presence of your Heavenly Father where your faith comes to fruition.

Praise the Lord, all you Gentiles! Laud Him, all you peoples! For His merciful kindness is great toward us.
Psalm 117:1-2

> We praise God because of His mercy. We are not judged for our deeds but for our faith in Jesus. We are considered God's people when we accept Jesus as our Savior.

This is the day the Lord has made; we will rejoice and be glad in it.
Psalm 118:24

> This was written praising Jesus' entry into Jerusalem. The people cheered for Him. We, too, should feel joy each day because He is with us daily. Take every opportunity to bring Him glory each day.

Happy are those who keep His decrees and seek Him with all their heart.
Psalm 119:2

> So many people today deal with anxiety and depression. Well, here's the cure; live according to God's commands and seek Him for love, companionship, and guidance.

Thy word I have hid in my heart, that I might not sin against You.
Psalm 119:11

> How do we evolve into better Christians? We read God's Word; think on it; and use it to fight temptations to sin. Make God's Word your desire. Hide it in your heart.

Let me understand the teaching of your precepts. Direct me in the path of your commands.
Psalm 119:27,35

God gives us rules but also, the Holy Spirit to teach us how to walk and to give us strength to keep from falling.

Before I was afflicted, I went astray, but now I keep your word.
Psalm 119:67

Sometimes we learn the hard way that God 's ways are for our good. We are forgiven when we sin but often, we have to suffer the consequences.

Thy word is a lamp unto my feet and a light unto my path.
Psalm 119:105

When you don't know what steps to take in a matter, go to God's Word for direction. It will shed light in any situation.

In my distress I cried to the Lord, and He heard me. Deliver my soul, O Lord, from lying lips and a deceitful tongue.
Psalm 120:1-2

As you live for Jesus, you will encounter opposition; mocking, lying, false accusations. Just count on it. But when you do, run to God in prayer for help. Our God is the best defense.

He who keep Israel shall neither slumber nor sleep.
Psalm 121:4

This is so comforting to know that God watches over me continually: when I work, play, drive, and even when I sleep. I have learned I don't need to fear. God keeps a watchful eye on me.

Pray for the peace of Jerusalem; may those who love you be secure. For the sake of my brothers and friends I will say, "Peace be with you."
Psalm 122:6,8

Unto You, I lift my eyes, O You who dwell in the heavens. Behold, as the eyes of a servant look to the hand of the master...
Psalm 123:1-2

In all we do, we should be looking to God for direction. We should be like a servant waiting on the signal from his master. Don't enter into anything without prayer, and wait for an answer.

Our help is in the name of the Lord, Maker of heaven and earth.
Psalm 124:8

We hear the scriptures repeat that God is our source of help. Let's get it and go to Him first when we need help. This verse brings out that it is His name that gives victory. That's why it is important to call upon Jesus in your prayer. There is power in His name.

Those who trust in the Lord are like Mount
Zion. It cannot be shaken; it remains
forever.
Psalm 125:1

> You do not have strong faith until you start exercising
> your faith and trust. God will arrange those situations
> that look hard or impossible so you will learn to trust
> Him. When you do, you will see miracles and your
> faith will become solid like Mount Zion.

Those who sow in tears shall reap in joy.
Psalm 126:5

> The word sow refers to sharing the Gospel. You may
> give up friends and being in vogue to share your faith,
> but that is why you're here. But God is faithful to the
> faithful, and you will reap joy.

It is useless to rise up early, to sit up late, to eat
the bread of sorrows, for He gives His beloved sleep.
Psalm 127:2

> This is not saying don't get up in time for work or
> school. It is referring to staying awake worrying how
> we get the task done. God will guide us and go with us
> to fulfill His plans for us. Pray, obey, and get some rest.

Blessed are all who fear the Lord, who walk in His ways. You will eat the fruit of your labors; blessings and prosperity will be yours.
Psalm 128:1

> This is advice on how to succeed and have a good life; honor and respect God, obey His word. You will be blessed and avoid pitfalls.

Let all those who hate Zion be put to shame and turned back.
Psalm 129:5

> Zion refers to God's people, Israel, and those who love Jesus. Let your heart be guided by the Holy Spirit to love those that God loves.

Hope in the Lord; for with the Lord there is mercy, and with Him is abundant redemption.
Psalm 130:7

> Mercy is not getting what you deserve but receiving a break, so to speak. And redemption means the cost is covered. Jesus' blood paid for our sin so we can enter God's presence and receive His favor not judgement. So put your faith in Him.

Lord, my heart is not haughty, nor my eyes lofty. Neither do I concern myself with great matters, not things too profound for me.
Psalm 131:1

God does not want us to walk around doubting our abilities, but this is emphasizing don't be arrogant and boastful. Know your limitations and develop your strengths and God given abilities. Then you won't need to brag. Your successes will be enough.

I will not give sleep to my eyes or slumber to my eyelids, until I find a place for the Lord...
Psalm 132:4-5

The place the Lord wants in your life is First Place. When you make Him number one everything else will fall into place.

Behold how good and how pleasant it is for brethren to dwell together in unity.
Psalm 133:1

> God created us to live together in harmony. that means helping each other, encouraging one another, and forgiving one another. It starts with you. If you sense disharmony with friends, check your attitude and heart. Ask the Holy Spirit to give you the mind and heart of God.

Behold, bless the Lord, all you servants of the Lord, who stand by night in the house of the Lord.
Psalm 134:1

> Praise focuses on the attributes of God: all powerful, all present, all knowing, all loving, kind. When you get this down into your heart, you won't have anxiety, worry, fear, or doubts. When you can't fall asleep, "stand by night" and praise God.

He causes the vapors to ascend from the ends of the earth; He makes lightning for the rain; He brings the wind out of His treasuries.
Psalm 135:7

We can complain on and on about the weather and climate change. God is in control, and He is not wringing His hands and waiting for puny man to fix this. Pray for rain, and cooler weather but what we need is revival of hearts and spiritual healing. Praise Him for the seasons, storms and sun.

For His mercy endures forever.
Psalm 136:1-26

This phrase is repeated twenty-six times in this psalm. It points out that no matter how many times we sin, God's mercy is available. Confess your sin and you will be forgiven. His mercy endures forever.

Those who carried us away captive asked of us a song, and those who plundered us required mirth.
Psalm 137:3

This is heartbreaking to think about. Jerusalem was taken captive by the Babylonians and the conquerors asked them to sing songs about it. They were defeated and in fear, but God strengthened them and eventually they were free. Like them, we too will go through hard experiences beyond our control. Stay faithful and God will not forsake you but strengthen you to bear your situation.

The Lord will perfect that which concerns me.
Psalm 138:8

What are your concerns or worries? Take it up with God in prayer. What troubles you is easy for God to fix, but you must lay it out before Him and trust that, "He will perfect what concerns you."

O Lord, You have searched me and know me.
You know my sitting down and my rising
up; You understand my thought afar off.
Psalm 139:1-2

This makes it pretty clear; we can't hide anything from
God. He sees every move you make and know your
thoughts and understands you better than you do.
What He wants from you is complete humility and
honesty before Him. He is your best friend and will
never leave you no matter what.

You formed my inward parts; You covered
me in my mother's womb. I will praise You,
for I am fearfully and wonderfully made.
Psalm 139:13-14

Two things here: God intentionally made you with
talents and abilities. God has plans for each unborn
child. You are fearfully and wonderfully made. Take
care of your body. It is an amazing gift.

How precious also, are Your thoughts to me, O God! How great is the sum of them!
Psalm 139:17

> It's hard to imagine that God thinks about me more times than there are grains of sand. Never feel forgotten. God thinks about you all day and all night.

Search me, O God, and know my heart; Try me, and know my anxieties; And see if there is any wicked way in me, and lead me in the way everlasting.
Psalm 139:23-24

> Do you want to get closer to God and have His power and blessings in your life? Pray this prayer with all your heart and you will be on your way to a transformed life but be prepared for what God will reveal.

I know that the Lord secures justice for the poor and upholds the cause of the needy.
Psalm 140:12

> Does your heart ache for those who are poor and without comforts? If you are filled with God's spirit it should. Pray about blessing someone who is in need.

Let my prayer be set before you as incense, the lifting of my hands as an evening sacrifice.
Psalm 141:2

What a lovely image! Our prayers reach God as a sweet fragrance. He is pleased to hear from you. Don't be afraid to lift your hands to reach up to God when you pray. All worship is a sacrifice or offering and shows your gratitude to Your Heavenly Father.

Set a guard over my mouth; keep a watch over the door of my lips.
Psalm 141:3

We should pray this before each time we speak. Our words bring consequences and cannot be taken back. We are told our words should be 'gracious (kind, building one another up); seasoned with salt (always revealing God's truth). Always consider this before you speak: Is it true? Is it kind? Is it necessary? Is it edifying?

Let not your heart be drawn to any evil thing, to practice wicked works with men who work iniquity.
Psalm 141:4

I pray daily you will have discernment and recognize what is good and what is evil, and that you will have wisdom to flee friends and activities that are not bringing you closer to God. Why follow the road to destruction?

Let the righteous strike me; It shall be kindness. And let him rebuke me; It shall be as oil; Let me not refuse it.
Psalm 141:5

No one naturally likes correction or rebuke but if you are submitted to God, you should be humble and wise enough to accept it. Sometimes it comes from people we know. This scripture says one who is righteous. Be humble. Take correction. If you do, it will eventually feel soothing to your soul like oil allowing you to break free from what is not godly.

I cried out to the Lord with my voice; with my voice to the Lord, I make my supplication. I pour out my complaint before Him; I declare my trouble.
Psalm 142:1-2

David knew trouble and despair but he also, knew where to go for help. Many psalms start out with despair or anxiety but after going to God, they end in hope...verse 7 "You shall deal bountifully with me." Don't stay "down." Look up!

Cause me to hear Your lovingkindness in the morning for in You do I trust.
Psalm 143:8

In this Psalm, David is in the depths of despair; he describes himself as crushed, overwhelmed, dead, in darkness. He cried out to God because he knew God is faithful. Sometimes we go through times like this but ask that you would hear His voice.

Lord, what is man, that You take knowledge of him? Or the son of man that You are mindful of him? Man is like a breath; His days are like a passing shadow.
Psalm 144:3-4

> We are not on the earth for very long. Life is relatively short compared with eternity. But you are not insignificant. God takes notice of what you do and cares about what you are going through. You are important to God.

Happy are the people whose God is the Lord!
Psalm 144:15

> Here is the key to true happiness; make God your Lord. In other words, quit living to satisfy your desires and submit to the Holy Spirit. Give each day to God in prayer and ask that He would take control of your desires, time and thoughts.

The Lord is near to all who call upon Him, to all who call upon Him in truth.
Psalm 145:18

> I don't know who you want to stay near but I'll take the Lord; the one who can fulfill my desires, preserve me in trouble, and bless me (verses 20, 21, 22). Ask Him to show you His care for you.

Happy is he who has the God of Jacob for his help.
Psalm 146:5

> The rest of this Psalm gives reasons why: He made Heaven and Earth. He executes justice, feeds the hungry, frees prisoners, opens blind eyes, loves the righteous, watches over the fatherless. You can trust and exalt God, or you can doubt God and the Bible and trust in what?

The Lord watches over the strangers; He relieves the fatherless and widow.
Psalm 146:9

> This scripture has been a comfort to me. God loves those who come here and don't know anyone (strangers). We need to be friendly and benevolent to those who come here for help. As a single mom the second part gave me comfort to know God saw me and He did always meet my needs.

He heals the broken hearted and binds up their wounds.
Psalm 147:3

> We often hear people question God when their hearts have been broken. In this life we will have heartache because we have free will and we are not all living the way God planned. We will lose loved ones, be rejected and suffer pain. But God will bind up your wounds and give you strength to go on. In time, you will feel His renewal and have joy and victory over your trouble. I know. It happened to me.

Great is the Lord, and mighty in power; His understanding is infinite. The Lord lifts up the humble; He casts the wicked to the ground.
Psalm 147:5-6

God is in control. There is no limit to His power or His knowledge of who we are. Many times, it is stated that God wants us to be humble. Don't be a bragger or boast of your accomplishments.

Give God the credit for your successes and He will lift you up. You don't have to do it.

Praise the Lord!
Psalm 148:1

Who should praise the Lord? This psalm goes on to list those: angels, hosts, sun and moon, stars and light, heaven, water, sea creatures, etc. All of creation is made by God to show His glory and give praise. Praise Him for something today.

The Lord takes pleasure in His people; He will beautify the humble with salvation.
Psalm 149:4

The Psalm again tells us to sing, dance, and praise God. Then it states that He is pleased with us and will give us beauty. This beauty isn't outward but in our soul. When we receive salvation, we must be humble and give up our will. Then God puts His spirit in you and that is the beauty. Pray that you will be humble and let God guide your life. Then you will sing and dance.

Let everything that has breath praise the Lord!
Psalm 150:6

This last psalm exhorts all of creation to rejoice and sing, dance and praise God. Praise to God develops a grateful heart. Take time each day to thank God for something and praise Him for His abundant blessings that He gives us each day. We have been given so much. Look around. We have been favored.

The fear of the Lord is the beginning of wisdom, but fools despise wisdom and instruction.
Proverb 1:7

> The book of Proverbs (wisdom) starts out very clearly. You can get degrees and honors, but real wisdom begins when we recognize and honor God. Don't get blinded by your pride You need God.

So are the ways of everyone who is greedy of gain; it takes away the life of its owner.
Proverbs 1:19

> Greed is a sin and destroys your conscience. Know when "it" is enough and give God thanks. Be grateful for all you have.

Fools hate knowledge.
Proverbs 1:22

> Take advantage of your education and learn all you can in school and from God's Word. You are not a fool.

Then, they will call on me, but I will not answer; They will seek me diligently, but they will not find me.
Proverbs 1:28

If you keep ignoring God's prompting and correction, He will leave you. Listen to His voice, humbly obey.

Whoever listens to me will dwell safely, and will be secure, without fear of evil.
Proverbs 1:33

This scripture has been an encouragement to me knowing I am safe in my home and wherever I am. I don't fear evil. I am certain God is my bodyguard.

He guards the path of justice, and preserves the way of His saints.
Proverbs 2:8

Justice means following the law. If we follow God's laws, we are preserved or protected. If we don't, we leave an opening to hurt and harm.

Discretion will preserve you; understanding will keep you to deliver you from evil.
Proverbs 2:11-12

> Modesty is another word for discretion. We are not to display ourselves physically or verbally as loose or immoral. It will lead you to temptation and destructive behavior. Stand strong against the trends. Dare to be different.

(Discretion) delivers you from the immoral woman, from the seductress who flatters with her words...for her house leads down to death...
Proverbs 2:16-18

> There are many warnings about the seduction of immoral women. Men, be on the alert. Don't fall for their flattery. Women be on guard as well. Men will promise you everything. Also, make sure you do not entice men by your dress and coyness. You have a big responsibility not to stumble a brother in the Lord to stumble.

Trust in the Lord with all your heart and lean not to your own understanding; in all your ways acknowledge Him, and He will direct your paths.
Proverbs 3:5

> This says it all about living. Ask God into your every day and ask Him to direct your steps. Recognize He is guiding you and acknowledge His presence.

Fear the Lord and depart from evil. It will be health to your flesh and strength to your bones.
Proverbs 3:7-8

> Honoring God and running from sin affects us spiritually, mentally, and physically. People run to doctors when they should run to God.

Honor the Lord with your possessions, and with the first of your increase.
Proverbs 3:9

> When we realize all we have comes from God, and He never runs out of blessing, sharing should come naturally. It is something God trusts us to do. Hebrews 13:16 says, "Do not forget to do good and to share, for with such sacrifices God is well pleased."

Whom the Lord loves He corrects just like a father the son in whom He delights.
Proverbs 3:12

> Troubles come into our lives because this is Earth, not Heaven. Sometimes it comes from the devil to keep us from doing good and obeying God. Sometimes it's consequences for behavior that is detrimental. But sometimes it is God saying, "Stop what you're doing."

Happy is the man who finds wisdom, and the man who gains understanding.
Proverbs 3:13

> This is talking about God's wisdom as found in the Bible especially this book of Proverbs. This verse promises if we follow or gain God's wisdom, we will find happiness. The following verses expound that God's wisdom is more valuable than silver or rubies. It brings life and fulfillment. We are so fooled by ads that promise if you buy more stuff, you'll be happy. Don't believe that. God is the real thing: knowing God.

They will be life to your soul and grace to
your neck. Then you will walk safely in
your way and your foot will not stumble.
Proverbs 3:22-23

> Again, this is a promise if we seek God's wisdom in all
> our plans, our paths will be peaceful, beautiful, and safe.
> Don't go forward without asking God for guidance.

Do not withhold good from those whom it
is due, when it is in your power to do so.
Proverbs 3:27

> This one gets to me. Never say you're too busy to give
> someone a hand, money, or encouragement. God put
> you in their path for a reason.

Do not envy the oppressor and choose none
of his ways.
Proverbs 3:31

> Don't be tempted to use worldly ways to get ahead. It
> may be tempting when you see worldly people prosper
> while you are working hard. But in due time, God will
> reward you, and you will not have to fear consequences
> of bad behavior.

Surely, He scorns the scornful, but gives grace to the humble.
Proverbs 3:34

To scorn someone is to look at them with distain, God wants us to look at all people as His creation. Think about how you could help that person instead of judging them. Be humble. God has blessed you.

Do not enter the path of the wicked, and do not walk the way of evil.
Proverbs 4:14

When God says, "Do not!" we better listen. Verses 15-16 go on to tell us that the intention of evil is to harm us. You know the difference. Don't play with danger: You will suffer.

But the path of the just is like a shining sun, that shines ever brighter unto the perfect day.
Proverbs 4:18

Our lives as Christians gets better and better the longer we know Jesus. We will have struggles, but with Jesus as our constant company we see the light of victory. We look forward to the perfect day when we will see Him face-to-face.

The way of the wicked is like darkness; they do not know what makes them stumble.
Proverbs 4:19

Did you ever notice how dark bars and clubs are? This may reflect that the people there don't want to see their dark deeds. Also, they never take responsibility for their trouble. They run from the light.

My son, give attention to my words; Incline your ear to my sayings; Do not let them depart from your eyes; Keep them in the midst of your heart; For they are life to those who find them, and health to all their flesh.
Proverbs 4:20-22

It's pretty important to memorize and know how to apply God's Word to our lives. We will have a more abundant life and stay healthier. I believe this. I feel I have experienced this truth in my life.

Keep your heart with all diligence, for out of it springs the issues of life.
Proverbs 4:23

> I always took this as a warning not to be led by whims and romantic emotions. We can control letting our hearts go. Let God give you the desires of your heart.

Put away from you a deceitful mouth and put perverse lips far from you.
Proverbs 4:24

> Now here's something we can control— What we say. It should always be true, honest, and clean.

Ponder the path of your feet, and let your ways be established. Do not turn to the right or to the left; remove your foot from evil.
Proverbs 4:26-27

> Think about your actions. They become patterns. Let them become established patterns to please God. Don't even turn or compromise a little. It will get you off the path of God's favor and plan for your life.

The lips of an immoral woman drip honey and her mouth is smoother than oil; but in the end she is bitter as wormwood, and sharp as a two-edged sword.
Proverbs 5:3-4

There are many warnings against falling into immoral sex. It is a big temptation and there will be many who try to seduce you. But this warning tells us to use wisdom. The result of seduction leaves you bitter and cut apart. Your heart will be broken.

My son, if you become a surety for your friend, if you have shaken hands in pledge for a stranger, you are snared by the words of your mouth.
Proverbs 6:1-2

This is referring to accepting responsibility for a friend's debt. Don't do it unless you are willing to pay the debt. But also, be careful about endorsing someone you don't know well. You may be leading someone to disaster.

Go to the ant you sluggard! Consider her
ways and be wise.
Proverbs 6:6-7

> This is an illustration of wisdom by a small creature to
> be productive and work hard. When given opportunity,
> they gather and store up food for winter. We too,
> should work are hardest when given opportunity. God
> trusts you to always do your best. Don't slack off.

These six things the Lord hates, Yes, seven
are an abomination to Him:
A proud look,
A lying tongue,
Hands that shed innocent blood,
A heart that devises wicked plans,
Feet that are swift in running to evil,
A false witness who speaks lies,
And one who sows discord among brethren.
Proverbs 6:16-19

> So…be humble, be kind, be honest, seek peace and run
> from evil.

My son, keep your father's command, and do not forsake the law of your mother. Bind them continually upon your neck. When you roam, they will lead you; when you sleep, they will keep you.
Proverbs 6:20-22

Do you want to walk easily through your day and have a good night's sleep? Then, seek God, study His commands, and embrace them as your guide. Then your days will go smoothly, and you can sleep peacefully.

The commandment is a lamp, and the law a light.
Proverbs 6:23

Some people rebel against God and say the Bible is full of "Thou shalt nots" that keep us from fun. But this tells us it is as a lamp that lights up the right way to go. Don't be too proud to admit you may need some guidance.

People do not despise the thief if he steals to satisfy himself when he is starving. Yet when he is found, he must restore sevenfold.
Proverbs 6:30-31

> God's Word teaches us to be merciful to those who are hurting. Poverty can make one desperate. We are to be compassionate, but also, hold accountability.

Whoever commits adultery with a woman lacks understanding. He who does destroys his own soul.
Proverbs 6:32

> It seems like this message is repeated a lot. Maybe, it's because it is a constant temptation in our world today that treats sex like a sport. It is a distortion of what God planned for a loving committed union. Satan always tries to present a counterfeit. Sex outside of marriage will come at a price instead of being a blessing.

My son, keep my words and treasure my commands within you. Keep my commands and live, and my law as the apple of your eye.
Proverbs 7:1-2

This chapter starts out with this solemn entreating of learning God's Word and keeping it. The rest of chapter seven describes the devices of sexual predators and their crafty ways. Then it ends with a stern warning that it will lead to wounds, destruction, and hell. God is trying to keep us safe. Obey God's laws! Obey civil laws too!

All my words in my mouth are with righteousness. Nothing crooked or perverse is in them.
Proverbs 8:8

This proverb personified wisdom, but we can apply this to ourselves. Righteousness means conforming to God's will and doing what is wise. Let's do our best to be like Christ and less like this world in our words and deeds.

The fear of the Lord is to hate evil, pride and arrogance and the evil way and a perverse mouth.
Proverbs 8:13

> "The fear of the Lord"…these words are often misunderstood. We are not to be afraid of God or His wrath. We are loved and forgiven. The word fear means to reverence God's authority and hate what He hates, which is evil.

I love those who love me, and those who seek me diligently will find me.
Proverbs 8:17

> This is the answer to those non-believers who doubt salvation is in Christ alone. This verse tells us if one is sincere in their search for God, they will find the truth…Jesus.

*When He prepared the heaven, I was there,
When He drew the circle on the face of the
deep, when He established the clouds above,
when He strengthened the fountains of
the deep...*
Proverbs 8:27-28

These verses are referring to creation, and Jesus (or
wisdom) was there. This is proof of Jesus being part
of the Trinity. Also, two scientific facts are mentioned:
the earth is round, and there are fountains of water
beneath the sea.

*Blessed are those who keep my ways. Hear my
instruction and be wise, and do not distain it.*
Proverbs 8:32-33

Why do we keep hearing this message? Maybe it really
is important.

*Don't rebuke a scoffer lest he hate you;
Rebuke a wise man, and he will love you.*
Proverbs 9:8

People who don't take correction are prideful and
foolish. A wise person recognizes he has faults and is
humble and grateful for correction. Be wise.

A foolish woman is clamorous; She sits at the door of her house...to call those who pass by...Whoever is simple, let him turn in here...But he does not know that the dead are there that her guests are in the depths of hell.
Proverbs 9:13,14,15,16,18

Sinful behavior is made out to look fun and inviting (drinking, drugs, immorality). But the truth is the foolish, or simple, fall for this allurement. Once caught, you are on a downward road. Stay strong in the convictions of your heart. You know what God requires of you.

He who has a slack hand becomes poor, but the hand of the diligent makes rich.
Proverbs 10:4

God gives us strong bodies and good minds. We are expected to use them to work, and He promises to reward our diligence.

The memory of the righteous is blessed.
The memory of the wicked will rot.
Proverbs 10:7

As I am getting old enough to die, I do hope what I have done on Earth will be remembered as a blessing. Try to do good every day. It is better to be missed because you were good than have your departure be a relief because you were a hindrance.

He who walks in integrity walks securely
but he who perverts his ways will become
known.
Proverbs 10:9

When you are honest in all you say and do, you can walk freely without fear of being found out. Your honesty is your defense. But those who lie or sneak have to worry about when they will be caught. Honesty brings real freedom.

("When you speak the truth, it becomes part of your past; when you lie, it becomes part of your future." -Ben DeHaven)

*The mouth of the righteous is a well of life,
but violence covers the mouth of the wicked.
Hatred stirs up strife, but love covers sins.
Proverbs 10:11-12*

Our words are so powerful. We can give encouragement and hope to someone, or we can destroy them and their reputation. We have a great responsibility, every time we open our mouths.

*The blessings of the Lord makes rich and
He adds no sorrow with it.
Proverbs 10:22*

God gives us spiritual and material blessings. When God gives, there is no striving or regret. Our response should always be thanks.

*The righteous will never be removed, but
the wicked will not inhabit the earth.
Proverbs 10:30*

This is a promise. If you are in Christ, you are considered righteous. God will not let you be destroyed by evil doers. The wicked may look like they are gaining ground, but in the end, they shall not have victory.

The lips of the righteous know what is acceptable.
Proverbs 10:32

It's fun being with friends and clowning around. But ask the Holy Spirit to teach you what is pleasing to God and refrain from coarse language and suggestive innuendos.

When pride comes, then comes shame; but with the humble is wisdom.
Proverbs 11:2

Don't toot your own horn. It is always best to take compliments graciously by saying a humble, "thank you" and remember it is God who gives us the abilities to succeed. So give Him a "thank you," as well.

The integrity of the upright will guide them, but perversity of the unfaithful will destroy them.
Proverbs 11:3

Determine to be honest in all you do, and you won't be a loser.

A talebearer reveals secrets, but he who is a faithful spirit conceals a matter.
Proverbs 11:13

It is so tempting to share something; gossip or something personal told to you. But remember you have been given another person's trust. Hold onto the information because it was meant for you. Be worthy of another's trust.

Where there is no councel, the people fall...
Proverbs 11:14

We can hear directly from God in prayer and through His Word. But sometimes we need to go to godly counselors (professionals, parents, friends). Getting others to look at our situations can give insight and wisdom and direct us to the right plan of action.

As a ring of gold in a swine's snout, so is a lovely woman who lacks discretion.
Proverbs 11:22

I really don't like Hollywood awards shows. You see beautiful talented women degrading themselves by wearing provocative clothing for attention. The inner character cannot be changed by outward ornamentation.

There is one who scatters yet increase more; and there is one who withholds more than is right, but it leads to poverty. The generous soul will be made rich, and he who waters will be watered himself.
Proverbs 11:24-25

> I learned you can't out-give God. He trusts you to let go of your material possessions and give generously to those in need. You will be surprised. "God will supply all your needs." Philippians 4:19

The fruit of the righteous is a tree of life, and he who wins souls is wise.
Proverbs 11:30

> The "tree of life" refers to our eternal life. When we bring others to a saving knowledge of Jesus we will have great reward. Matthew 28:19 says, "Go therefore and make disciples of all the nations."

Whoever loves instruction loves knowledge,
but he who hates correction is stupid.
Proverbs 12:1

> When you think you know it all, it's probably that you
> know very little. There's so much more than we think.
> Be humble; be willing to learn from others. Don't be
> stupid!

A good man obtains favor from the Lord...
Proverbs 12:2

> Often, I pray God shows you favor. Here we see God's
> will. Goodness is a fruit of the Holy Spirit working
> inside you.

An excellent wife is the crown of her
husband, but she who causes shame is like
rottenness in his bones.
Proverbs 12:4

> Wow! The wrong mate can actually make you rot but
> a wife who fears God will only bring good and honor.
> Prepare yourself to be a godly wife or husband by
> knowing God and putting Him first in your life. Don't
> be caustic.

A righteous man regards the life of his animal, but the tender mercies of the wicked are cruel.
Proverbs 12:10

> Proverbs often teach by contrast and comparison. Here we see a kind person who is kind even to an animal. Back then animals were used for working on farms. But a wicked person doesn't even know what kindness is. Always be willing to be kind even in conflict.

There is one who speaks like the piercings of a sword, but the tongue of the wise promotes health.
Proverbs 12:18

> Our words can do so much good or irreparable harm. If you are wise, you will speak words of encouragement and love rather than sarcasm and criticism. No smack talk.

Deceit is in the heart of those who devise evil, but counselors of peace have joy. No great trouble will overtake the righteous but the wicked shall be filled with evil.
Proverbs 12:20-21

> Do we get it? To be free from trouble and have joy, flee evil and choose peace and God's path of righteousness.

Anxiety in the heart of man causes depression, but a good word makes it glad.
Proverbs 12:25

> This is the new plague...anxiety. The cure is within reach. We are to input the positive word of God and put our faith in Our Heavenly Father to hear us when we call for help. Philippians 4:6 says, "Be anxious for nothing but in everything by prayer and supplication with thanksgiving let your requests be make known to God; and the peace of God which surpasses understanding will guard your heart and mind."

The righteous should choose his friends carefully, for the way of the wicked leads them astray.
Proverbs 12:26

Take this to heart. Sometimes you have to part ways with friends who do not love Jesus. You will only be led to compromising your values. Love them; witness to them; pray for them. But don't spend time or put your confidence in them. You will be pulled down.

A wise son heeds his father's instruction, but a scoffer does not listen to rebuke.
Proverbs 13:1

No one likes to be corrected by their parents, especially as we get older. But if we're wise, we heed. After all, no one cares more about your success and happiness than your parents.

He who guards his mouth preserves his life, but he who opens wide his lips shall have destruction.
Proverbs 13:3

> God keeps telling us we don't always have to speak out. Know when to share your opinion and when to shut your mouth. Pray for wisdom. If your words will promote good, great! But don't stir things up. Colossians 4:6 says, "Let your words be graciously seasoned with salt (love and truth).

Righteousness guards him whose way is blameless, but wickedness overthrows the sinner.
Proverbs 13:6

> If you always do the right thing you don't have to watch your back. God will protect you and give you favor.

There is one who makes himself rich, yet has nothing; and one who makes himself poor yet has great riches.
Proverbs 13:7

This is a reminder that God trusts us with money, not to hang onto it, but that we freely give it to help others. Be sensitive to the Holy Spirit when He leads you to give. The riches you receive are being stored in heaven.

Wealth gained be dishonesty will be diminished, but he who gathers by labor will increase.
Proverbs 13:11

There's nothing wrong with working hard. Don't envy those who get rich by cheating others or taking advantage of them. God sees what they're doing. Work hard, and you will have all your needs met.

Hope deferred makes the heart sick, but when desire comes, it is a tree of life.
Proverbs 13:12

The first part is sad reality. As humans, we all have disappointments…some small and some big. When this happens, we need to put things into perspective. God is in control.

*He who walks with wise men will be wise,
but the companion of fools will be destroyed.
Proverbs 13:20*

> Don't waste your time and energy on those who are
> fools. (The fool has said in his heart there is no God.
> Psalm 14:1) People who don't know Jesus and don't
> have the Holy Spirit will not bring beneficial results.
> Seek Christian friends.

*A good man leaves an inheritance to his
children's children.
Proverbs 13:22*

> This reminds me how unselfish my father was. He
> didn't spend his money lavishly. He made himself
> comfortable, and that was enough. He unselfishly left
> money for his children, and I hope to do the same.

*Much good is in the fallow ground of the poor.
Proverbs 13:23*

> There are different ways I have looked at this. One,
> that we need to work hard when given the opportunity.
> The other is to look at your spiritual life. Is your heart
> hard to God's correction and leading? Allow God to
> break up your fallow ground and be conformed to the
> Lord Jesus Christ.

He who spares the rod hates his son, but he who loves him disciplines him promptly.
Proverbs 13:24

> Well, we all hate hearing this, but think about it. Your parents love you so much they are just trying to keep you from destruction. With humility, give thanks.

The righteous eats to the satisfying of his soul, but the stomach of the wicked shall be in want.
Proverbs 13:25

> We are body, mind and spirit. It is all connected. We need to feed our spirits as well as our bodies. Sometimes when I just want to eat, and I'm not really hungry, I ask myself and God, "What am I really missing?" It is usually needing to forgive someone, forgetting things of the past, or just spending some time in God's Word. That is what feeds our souls and brings satisfaction.

The wise woman builds her house, but the foolish pulls it down with her hands.
Proverbs 14:1

> Women have much influence in the home. If you want your home a happy, safe and nurturing place, give kind words. Be your family's cheerleader. Never berate or be sarcastic. Never say anything negative about them to anyone.

In the mouth of a fool is a rod of pride but the lips of the wise will preserve them.
Proverbs 14:3

> What do you think of someone who boasts or brags? Well God says he's a fool. Make sure you are humble even in success and victory.

Where no oxen are, the trough is clean; but much increase comes by the strength of an ox.
Proverbs 14:4

> I am pretty independent and find it easier to do tasks myself. But the labor is easier with others and sometimes they have better ideas and more knowledge. Strong friendships are built when you work alongside someone. God likes that.

A scoffer seeks wisdom and does not find it, but knowledge is easy to him who understands.
Proverbs 14:6

> A scoffer is one who mocks and is sarcastic. He is not teachable because he is self-centered. One who gains understanding needs to acknowledge he doesn't know it all.

Go from the presence of a foolish man.
Proverbs 14:7

The folly of fools is deceit.
Proverbs 14:8

Fools mock at sin.
Proverbs 14:9

> Ok. Now you can identify a fool. Make a wise choice for friends.

A good man will be satisfied from above,
Proverbs 14:14

There's peace and joy when you walk in God's will. Seek God every morning before you even step out of bed. Do His will each day, and you will have fulfillment.

The simple believes every word, but the prudent considers well his steps.
Proverbs 14:15

We receive so much information every day but always consider your sources. Not everything we read or hear on the news is true or correct. Ephesians 5:15says, "See that you walk circumspectly not as fools." Another way of saying this is "never assume." Check your sources.

A quick-tempered man acts foolishly...
Proverbs 14:17

Did you ever feel that after you lost it?

*In labor there is profit, but idle chatter
leads only to poverty.*
Proverbs 14:23

> Always do your best whether you see the fruit of your
> labor and even when you're tired. Your hard work will
> lead to reward.

*A sound heart is life to the body, and envy
is rottenness to the bones.*
Proverbs 14:30

> What we think does affect our bodies. Our brains
> produce chemical that can do us good or hurt us. Ask
> God each day to give you His perspective on all you
> will face that day, and don't dwell on the negative.

*He who oppresses the poor reproaches his
Maker, but he who honors Him has mercy
on the needy.*
Proverbs 14:31

> God expects us to defend the poor and give generously
> to their needs when we are able. Don't think that those
> who cheat or take advantage of them will get away with
> it. Do all you can to be kind and generous. Then you
> will know you are filled with God's Spirit.

A gentle answer turns away anger, but harsh words stir up wrath.
Proverbs 15:1

> The best way to end an argument is don't get in it. Let someone spout off until they have nothing left to say. Think of it as air blowing out of a balloon. "Don't take anything personally." Then, ask the Holy Spirit to give you kind words; be understanding of their feelings. Remember, by now he feels like a fool (Proverbs 14:17).

The eyes of the Lord are in every place, keeping watch on the evil and the good.
Proverbs 15:3

> I don't k now how He does it, but God never takes His eyes off you.

A wholesome tongue is a tree of life, but perverseness in it breaks the spirit.
Proverbs 15:4

> Our good, kind, and encouraging words give hope and life to others. But we can easily bring harm by using bad language, spewing bitterness and lies.

A fool despises his father's instruction, but he who receives correction is prudent.
Proverbs 15:5

> After 75 years of life, I wish I could go back and heed the instruction of my parents. Unfortunately, some of us have to learn our lessons the hard way. Now, I see their wisdom and loving care.

In the house of the righteous is much treasure; but the revenues of the wicked is trouble.
Proverbs 15:6

> Living a righteous life brings treasure money can't buy: God's presence, peace, freedom from guilt, and regrets. Wicked people may prosper while they're here, but they are missing out on true fulfillment.

A merry heart makes a cheerful countenance, but sorrow of the heart the spirit is broken.
Proverbs 15:13

> Emotions are useful. Joy and cheer lift up our hearts to overflow to others, but sorrow is used to break our wills. Bring us to repentance, and cause us to draw nearer to God.

All the days of the afflicted are evil, but he who has a merry heart has a continual feast.
Proverbs 15:15

> To have a happy heart, feast or focus on the love, joy, and promises of God. Stay away from evil doers, false teachers, and those who oppose God.

Better is a little with the fear of the Lord, than great treasure with trouble.
Proverbs 15:16

> What God provides, be thankful for. He gives us everything we need, not everything we want. He withholds things that would not be beneficial. Say, "Thank you."

The way of a lazy man is like a hedge of thorns, but the way of the upright is a highway. Not putting out your best is being lazy. If you do your best God will your efforts.
Proverbs 15:19

Without counsel, plans go awry, but in the multitude of counselors they are established.
Proverbs 15:22

We need to be humble and realize we don't have all the answers. It's good to go to wise counselors for their wisdom and knowledge.

A man has joy by the answer of his mouth and a word spoken in due season how good it is.
Proverbs 15:23

Do you want joy? Speak positively to others. Give compliments freely, encouragement with compassion, and advice with God's wisdom from His word.

The Lord will destroy the house of the proud, but He will establish the boundary of the widow.
Proverbs 15:25

> Proud people don't acknowledge God as their source for success. They like to think their accomplishments were of their own doing. But a widow had to depend on God for provision and comfort. God rewards our faith and need for Him.

The heart of the righteous studies how to answer, but the mouth of the wicked pours forth evil.
Proverbs 15:28

> What comes out of your mouth reveals what's in your heart. Don't just blurt out smack or sarcasm, which comes from jealousy or arrogance. Study God's Word and speak kindness. Study how to speak, pleasing to God.

A good report makes the bones healthy.
Proverbs 15:30

> Now, here's a scripture to ward off osteoporosis. Research does show that the mind, body and spirit do influence each other. RX: Colossians 3:2 says, "Set your mind on things above, not on things of earth."

Commit your words to the Lord and your thought will be established.
Proverbs 16:3

> Commit everything you do to glorify God, and He will bless your efforts and inspire your thinking.

When a man's ways please the Lord, He makes even his enemies to be at peace with him.
Proverbs 16:7

> I love this promise. We are to forgive everyone whether they want it or not. The result is you will have peace for pleasing the heart of God.

The highway of the upright avoids evil; the one who guards his way protects his life.
Proverbs 16:17

> As Christians and people with wisdom, we should walk away from any evil: friends, places, movies, websites. We are saved, but we can be pulled into darkness. Guard your heart, protect your mind, and watch carefully where you step.

Pride goes before destruction, and a haughty spirit before a fall.
Proverbs 16:18

> This is a good one to keep in mind. Never think you are better than anyone else. You may trip and fall as you walk with your nose up in the air.

Pleasant words are like honeycomb, sweetness to the soul and health to the bones.
Proverbs 16:24

> Pleasant, kind, encouraging words are sweet in our mouths and sweet to the heart of the receiver. I think it may help ward off osteoporosis (?).

*A perverse man sows strife, and a whisperer
separates the best of friends.*
Proverbs 16:28

This is what we don't want to be like... a gossip or one who creates ill feelings between people. Why is it we humans love knowing gossip? It is our fallen nature. A good rule to follow is don't repeat a matter if it doesn't concern you and you are not a part of any solution. Consider if you would say this in front of the person you are talking about.

*The silver haired head is a crown of glory,
if it is found in the way of righteousness.*
Proverbs 16:31

Growing old with the Lord is glorious. The big word here is, "if." *If* you know Jesus as your Lord and Savior. I think of all He's done for me through the years, and I am so thankful. I know, I have never been alone, and He has lead me in paths of righteousness (Psalm23).

Better to be patient than powerful; better to have self-control than conquer a city.
Proverbs 16:32

> Wow! Politicians and world leaders need to heed this. We, too, need to let God's Spirit guide us and to be humble. You don't always have to win an argument or battle to show you are strong. Self-control takes trusting God for the outcome.

The lot is cast into the lap, but it's every decision is from the Lord.
Proverbs 16:33

> People who gamble don't know this. God controls everything. If you are meant to have wealth, He will guide you. You don't have to strive, cheat, or lose your dignity. I feel sorry for gamblers. Their hope is misplaced. Never say, "Good luck," say, "God's favor."

Better is a dry crust eaten in peace, than a house filled with feasting and conflict.
Proverbs 17:1

> Peace and love between family members is better than prosperity and greed in a home. Godly families enjoy God's blessings, and I'm sure better digestion.

*The refining pot is for silver and the furnace
for gold, but the Lord tests the heart.*
Proverbs 17:3

Impurities are removed from precious metals by high heat. There are times when we go through difficult circumstances and are faced with hard decisions. These are trials.

What we do and where we put our trust will come forth. Make your actions reflect your faith in God, and you will come out like gold... precious in the sight of God.

He who mocks the poor reproaches his Maker.
Proverbs 17:5

God wants us to be generous and kind to the poor. Don't snicker if someone is dressed in last year's fashion. Have empathy to those less fortunate and offer help.

Children's children are the crown of old men (and women), and the glory of children is their father.
Proverbs 17:6

Families are a gift from God, especially those who know Jesus. Michaelynn and George are like my shining crown on my head. They bring me joy, and fulfillment, and glory before the Lord as they honor Him. Having a godly father is something children can take pride and safety in as well. We are blessed.

He who covers a transgression seeks love, but he who repeats a matter separates friends.
Proverbs 17:9

Here we have it again, don't repeat gossip or share someone's shortcomings. We are tempted to do this, but it only creates bad feelings and hurts reputations. It also hurts you and gives you a reputation as a gossip.

A rebuke is more effective for a wise man than a hundred blows on a fool.
Proverbs 17:10

> If we are wise, we can take correction because we are wise enough to know we are not perfect and humble enough to be willing to take advice or criticism.
>
> We can always get better.

The beginning of strife is like releasing of water; Therefore, stop contention before a quarrel starts.
Proverbs 17:14

> You can't catch water with your fists, and you can't stop anger once a quarrel starts. How do you avoid this? Humility and giving up your rights to be heard, to convince, and to win.

Acquitting the guilty and condemning the just... both are detestable to the Lord.
Proverbs 17:15

> This is pretty strong language. Today our court system does just that. Those slick lawyers and unfair justices will be accountable eventually. We must trust God. There is not much justice on this planet.

A friend loves at all times.
Proverbs 17:17

Real friends are hard to come by and difficult to be. To be a friend is to stay by someone when you agree and disagree, do well and fail, are joyful and drowning in sorrow. Jesus is the one who stays by us no matter what.

A merry heart does good like a medicine.
Proverbs 17:22

Negative thoughts can actually make you sick, and some cancers are related to our emotions. You can't stop emotions, but you can direct your thinking which leads to emotions. Philippians 4:8 tells us to think on things that are good and virtuous. Watch what you read and view on the internet and TV. Don't poison your mind and then wonder why you aren't happy.

Even a fool is counted wise when he holds his peace, and a man of understanding is of a calm spirit.
Proverbs 17:27

Sometimes the wisest thing is to keep your mouth shut and keep your emotions under control.

A man who isolates himself seeks his own desires; he rages against all wise judgement.
Proverbs 18:1

> Sometimes people can be exhausting, and it's easier to be left alone. That is a very selfish attitude. The scripture suggests this and if you isolate, you don't listen to advice or judgement. You can always be right in your own eyes.

Fools have no interest in understanding; they want to air their own opinion.
Proverbs 18:2

> There are some people who are not fun to engage with. They never listen to what is being said and they interrupt conversations to give their "wisdom."

The words of a man's mouth are deep waters; the wellspring of wisdom is a flowing brook.
Proverbs 18:4

> I want my words to be refreshing and life-giving as a flowing brook. It takes studying God's Word for wisdom and submission to the Holy Spirit to keep from blurting out from my human reaction.

*Fool's words get them into constant quarrels;
they are asking for a beating.*
Proverbs 18:6

> Have you ever observed this? Some people just don't know when to "give it a rest." Use wisdom and know when to drop a subject.

*The name of the Lord is a strong tower; the
righteous run to it and are safe.*
Proverbs 18:10

> A tower is a place of safety and so is the name of the Lord, Jesus. There are many warnings in scriptures that tell us to call upon His name; every knee will bow at His name: the demons flee at His name. Call upon His name when you need help. Don't use it as a curse word when a problem occurs, cry it out as a prayer.

*Before destruction, the heart of a man is
haughty and before honor is humility.*
Proverbs 18:12

> Two things are here: if you are puffed up, you will get deflated; and if you are humble, God will bring honor and recognition.

The spirit of man will sustain him in sickness.
Proverbs 18:14

> Body, mind, and spirit work together. One affects the other. Sometimes someone feels tired or sick but there is no physical cause. It starts in emotions. Adversely, if you don't take care of your body, you can get depressed from lack of sleep or poor nutrition. A positive outlook can give you strength to overcome illness. "You are fearfully and wonderfully made."

The first one to plead his cause seems right,
until his neighbor comes and examines him.
Proverbs 18:17

> There are two sides to every story. Listen to both before you come to a conclusion and never takes sides. Just be empathetic with both.

A man who has friends must show himself friendly, but there is a friend who sticks closer than a brother.
Proverbs 18:24

> You make friends by showing an interest in someone. We all respond to a warm smile and kindness. Jesus is one friend who will never leave you nor disappoint you.

Wealth makes many friends, but the poor is separated from his friend.
Proverbs 19:4

> This is sad but true. Everyone wants to be with the rich and famous, but then it's hard to know who is a true friend and who wants something from you. People don't seek out poor people to be their friends even though they may be kinder and more sincere.

A false witness will not go unpunished, and he who speaks lies will not escape.
Proverbs 19:5

> God wants us to speak truth at all times. You will be embarrassed when lies are found out, so don't lie. Truth does not have to be defended.

The discretion of a man makes him slow to anger, and his glory is to overlook a transgression.
Proverbs 19:11

> When you develop good judgement, you will not show anger or hold onto past offenses. Just as God forgives and forgets our transgressions, we are to overlook the faults of others. Don't share them either.

A foolish son is the ruin of his father.
Proverbs 19:13

This refers to a son or daughter. Parents pour their hearts out; give generously of finances and use all their skills and resources to lead their children to success and fulfillment. This sacrificial love is hard to match. It is a sad thing when a child doesn't take advantage and do their best. It will break the hearts of the parents.

Listen to counsel and receive instructions, that you may be wise in your later days.
Proverbs 19:20

Life is a continual learning experience. In every new experience, ask God what He wants you to learn. It's not always easy admitting you don't know it all. Be teachable. Let God be your Wonderful Counselor.

The fear of the Lord leads to life, and he who has it will abide in satisfaction; He will not be visited with evil.
Proverbs 19:23

When we respect God and follow His instruction, we are blessed and receive God's favor. If you try to go it without Him, you are opening yourself up to evil which leads to destruction. Ask God to give you awareness of His goodness in your life.

Wine is a mocker, strong drink is a brawler, and whoever is lead astray by it is not wise.
Proverbs 20:1

The Bible never says don't drink, but there are many warnings that those who allow it to influence them are foolish, and it will lead to destruction.

It is honorable for a man to stop striving, since any fool can start a quarrel.
Proverbs 20:3

It is not our nature or popular to back down or take the high road and let someone else think they won an argument. But in God's eyes, you are the winner when you walk away. It's not an admission you agree. It's proof you are not a fool.

The righteous man walks in his integrity;
his children are blessed after him.
Proverbs 20:7

> Those words: righteous and integrity, refer to honesty, morality, just, and undivided. This is how we should live our lives before God. When we do, our paths are easy, and those we love reap our blessings.

Do not love sleep, lest you come to poverty,
open your eyes and you will be satisfied
with bread.
Proverbs 20:13

> Here is a warning not to be lazy but to get up and be willing to take opportunities to work. I know many successful people. None of them gained wealth by sitting back. It takes hard work.

Bread gained by deceit is sweet to a man,
but afterwards his mouth will be filled with
gravel.
Proverbs 20:17

> You will never get away with deceit, lying, stealing. It will eventually be brought into the open.

Do not say, "I will recompense evil." Wait for the Lord, and He will save you.
Proverbs 20:22

> God does not want us to "get back" at those who wrong us. Remember, we are to treat others as God treats us with mercy and forgiveness. Then, let God deal with those who have harmed you. He will. You are His child.

A man's steps are of the Lord; How can a man understand his own way?
Proverbs 20:24

> One of my favorite quick prayers is I Chronicles 4:10 (The Prayer of Jabez)
>
> Bless me, enlarge my area of influence, keep your hand on me, keep me from evil or causing pain.
>
> When God guides your steps, you can rest in every situation knowing God has you there for a reason. You may not understand why, but let God show you.

The Lord's lamp sheds light on a person's life.
Proverbs 20:27

God's Word is the lamp. Anything we do or say should be in line with God's commands and precepts. Check your thoughts and habits. Do they line up with God's teaching?

Blows that hurt cleanse away evil, as do stripes the inner depths of the heart.
Proverbs 20:30

Sometimes it takes pain, failure, or brokenness to get us to let go of sin.

Every way of man is right in his own eyes, but the Lord weighs the hearts.
Proverbs 21:2

You can do good, but if your motive is selfish, God sees. We are to do all things out of love for God. If it's the Lord, your work is selfless, sacrificial, and generous.

To do righteousness and justice is more acceptable to the Lord than sacrifice.
Proverbs 21:3

Choosing to do the right thing is what God wants from you. It makes Him happy to see you obey and give out His love. Some people think if they give money or help at church, it will make up for their bad behavior. Jesus' death is all we need to be acceptable to God, but to please His heart, we are to live a godly life. Remember, the Christian life is a relationship between you and your Heavenly Father. Stay close. Talk often.

Better to dwell in a corner of a housetop, than a house shared with a contentious woman.
Proverbs 21:9

This is a warning to young men not to pick a woman who is argumentative and a warning to women not to be so.

Whoever shuts his ears to the cry of the poor will also cry himself and not be heard.
Proverbs 21:13

> Not everyone is blessed financially, so if you are, you are trusted by God to give generously to those in need. We shouldn't be concerned with how much we can buy but how much we can give away.

A gift in secret pacifies anger, and a bribe behind the back, "strong wrath."
Proverbs 21:14

> Now, I'm not sure if this sounds godly, but it does work. Generosity and gifts certainly can smooth over hard feelings when given in the right attitude, love, and thoughtfulness.

The person who strays from common sense will end up in the company of the dead.
Proverbs 21:16

> We are born with common sense; knowing what is right; understanding consequences of actions. Use what God has given you to make right choices.

He who loves pleasure will be a poor man;
he who loves wine and oil will not be rich.
Proverbs 21:17

> God wants us to enjoy the fruit of our labor but don't squander it on frivolous pleasure and especially those things that can ruin your life.

There is desirable treasure and oil in the
dwelling of the wise, but a foolish man
squanders it.
Proverbs 21:20

> This is more advice not to spend your money foolishly. You may be rich today, but if you spend all your money, you are broke. Give to God and save up for the future.

He who guards his mouth and tongue keeps
his soul from trouble.
Proverbs 21:23

> We are reminded to watch what we say, again. God knows this is a real problem for us.
>
> A good rule is if it doesn't edify or encourage and if it isn't necessary, you don't need do say it.

*The horse is prepared for the day of battle,
but deliverance is of the Lord.*
Proverbs 21:31

> We are to do our best to fight spiritual battles: people
> who oppose us, temptations drugs, alcohol, sex, etc.,
> Use God's Word as your guide and then His Holy Spirit
> will come in and by His power you will be set free.

*A good name is to be chosen rather than great
riches; loving favor than silver and gold.*
Proverbs 22:1

> Who you are and how you treat others defines you
> and creates your reputation. Money has little value.
> It is character that is priceless. You can't buy a good
> reputation.

*A prudent man foresees evil and hides himself,
but the simple pass on and are punished.*
Proverbs 22:3

> Two things here: if anything seems wrong, avoid it
> (deeds, talk, activities); there will be consequences for
> them. So don't be stupid (simple).

Train up a child in the way he should go, and when he is old, he will not depart from it.
Proverbs 22:6

> This is God's promise to parents. If we teach our children and lead by example to love and obey God, even if they stray; they will remember God's Word and run to it for wisdom and strength eventually.

The rich rule over the poor and the borrower is servant to the lender.
Proverbs 22:7

> The first part is unfortunate but true. People with money often get into positions of control. But the second part is a warning not to borrow, especially money. You will be under the scrutiny of the lender.

He who has a generous eye will be blessed.
Proverbs 22:9

> This we have heard before. God wants us to give freely from our abundance. But also, when we have need, we are to put others first. Our generosity is of our money, time, and talents. Look for ways you can be generous today.

The lazy man says,"There is a lion outside!
I shall be slain in the streets!"
Proverbs 22:13

Excuses are just that. They don't get the job done. The best thing is just to get to work. A job done well is satisfying and a blessing to others.

Foolishness is bound up in the heart of a
child; The rod and correction will drive it
far from him.
Proverbs 22:15

We are God's children, and sometimes we do act foolishly. You can know God loves you when you go through chastisement and feel the blows for foolish and sinful behavior. God is like a good parent telling you, "Stop that!"

Incline your ear and hear the words of the
wise and apply your heart to knowledge.
Proverbs 22:17

Who are the wise? They are not on TV or the internet. The only true wisdom comes from God's Word. It is true. It never changes. Read the Bible daily for wisdom. Let it get into your heart. Share what you learn with others today.

Make no friendship with an angry man, and with a furious man do not go, lest you learn his ways.
Proverbs 22:24

> Be kind to all people but be selective who you spend time with. If your friends swear, are angry or critical, soon you will be too. Usually, bad company pulls you down. Rarely can you pull them up.

Do not be one of those who shakes hands in a pledge, one of those who is a surety for debts.
Proverbs 22:26

> This is financially sound advice. Never co-sign or assume someone else's debts. You can be in a position to lose all you own. People mean well, but stuff happens.

Do not overwork to be rich, because of your own understanding, cease.
Proverbs 23:4

> We should be grateful for our jobs, and always do our best, but trust God for your income. He will supply your needs. Philippians 6:19 says, "Don't let your focus be money but a job well done."

Do not speak in the hearing of a fool, for he despises the wisdom of your words.
Proverbs 23:9

> Psalm 14 tells us a fool is one who denies God. There is no use speaking God's truth to him. He won't get it.

Do not mix with winebibbers or gluttonous eaters of meat: for the drunkard and glutton will come to poverty.
Proverbs 23:20-21

> Our flesh is so strong, God has to continually warn us not to let food, alcohol or any lust control us. It will lead you on a downward slope. You won't be able to stop yourself from going down. Stay clear of these temptations. Don't become enslaved.

Eat honey, my son, for it is good, and honeycomb is sweet to the taste.
Proverbs 24:13-14

> God's wisdom should be sweet to our soul, and we should desire it more each day. God's wisdom brings us hope for the future even during difficult days.

Do not rejoice when your enemy falls, and do not let your heart be glad when he stumbles; lest the Lord see it and it displeases Him, and He turns away His wrath from him.
Proverbs 24:17-18

> I have a hard time with this. I'm tempted to be happy when some impatient driver passes me, and we both end up stopping at a light up the road. We need to show compassion and concern, even for those who are enemies or just "bug" us.

He who says to the wicked, "You are righteous," will be cursed by many nations.
Proverbs 24:24

> We live in a time when sin and wickedness are common and accepted behavior. Be sure, God is not winking at sin. We are to call it out and stand strong in the power of the Holy Spirit. Don't be afraid to speak against the evil, even when it is not popular.

Prepare your outside work, make it fit for yourself in the field; and afterward, build your house.
Proverbs 24:27

> This is good advice. Don't spend money on something before you are sure of your ability to earn enough to pay for it. We depend on credit too often. That is an irresponsible way to live.

A little sleep, a little slumber, a little folding of the hands to rest; so shall poverty come like a prowler, and your need like an armed man.
Proverbs 24:33

> God does not like slackers. They will not be rewarded. Colossians 3:23 says, "Whatever you do, do heartily as unto the Lord."

Take away the dross from silver, and it will go to the silversmith for jewelry. Take away the wicked from before the king, and his throne will be established in righteousness.
Proverbs 25:4-5

> You can't expect good to come when there is a presence of evil. Just as silver needs to be purified, so do we. Ask the Holy Spirit to show you what needs to be removed from your life, so you will be as shiny as silver.

Do not exalt yourself in the presence of the king, and do not stand in the place of the great; for it is better that he say to you, "Come up here," than you should be put lower.
Proverbs 25:6-7

> Let's remember to be humble and not assume, "I am the greatest." Take your victories with grace. Remember, "Without God I can do nothing."

Timely advice is lovely, like apples of gold in a silver basket.
Proverbs 25:11

> This is a picture of how precious good words are to those who are ready to listen. Be humble and listen to the wisdom of godly teachers, friends, and loved ones.

By long forbearance, a ruler is persuaded, and a gentle tongue breaks the bones.
Proverbs 25:15

> Our words are powerful when used with wisdom. This tells us we can be persuasive when we are consistent and speak with kindness and gentleness. Harsh words and a haughty attitude are not what wins people over. A gentle answer can end an argument.

Don't visit your neighbors too often, or you will wear out your welcome.
Proverbs 25:17

> I love how God gives practical advice. Most of us love company, and we need each other, but be sensitive to leave before someone wishes you would go.

If your enemy is hungry, give him food to eat, and if he's thirsty, give him water to drink; you will heap burning coals on his head and the Lord will reward you.
Proverbs 25:21

> This reminds us to be compassionate and giving even to those who hurt or oppose us. God will bless you. You will never be sorry you were kind.

A righteous man who falters before the wicked is like a murky spring and polluted well.
Proverbs 25:26

> This is a picture of what you are like if you compromise your witness for God because you are concerned about someone's ridicule or rebuff. Don't fear man, but glorify God.

Do not answer a fool according to his folly, lest you also be like him.
Proverbs 26:4

> Don't get engaged in a stupid argument or conversation. Just walk away.

As a dog returns to his own vomit, so a fool repeats his folly.
Proverbs 26:11

> "Folly" is described as foolishness or unprofitable behavior. If you're unhappy or frustrated, quit repeating what doesn't work. Ask God for His guidance and let Him guide your steps. You are not a fool. You are God's child.

Just as damaging as a mad man shooting a deadly weapon, is someone who lies to a friend and then says, "I was only joking."
Proverbs 26:18-19

Think about this. Killing is serious, and one who has no reason is irrational. Lying is just as serious to God, and it can destroy. Trying to justify it makes it worse. "Thou shalt not bear false witness." Truthfulness will keep you from much trouble.

Fervent lips with a wicked heart are like earthenware covered with silver dross.
Proverbs 26:23

Verses 24 and 25 go on to describe those who disguise hatred and deceit by speaking kindly and sweetly. They cover upon evil intent with flattery. Pray for discernment and wisdom and trust when the Holy Spirit nudges you to watch out.

Don't brag about tomorrow, since you don't know what the day will bring. Let someone else praise you, not your own mouth.
Proverbs 27:1-2

> We all want to be acknowledged for our achievements. Let someone else give the praise. No one likes a bragger, and you may be humbled the next time. This is especially true for those of us who play golf. Always give God the credit and be gracious in your achievements.

Faithful are the wounds of a friend, but the kisses of an enemy are deceitful.
Proverbs 27:6

> Honesty in relationships is paramount. Honest criticism or correction from someone who loves you is better than insincere flattery.

A person who is full refuses honey, but to the hungry soul, every bitter thing is sweet.
Proverbs 27:7

> This reminds me of this, "Input the positive, and the negative will go away." When we fill ourselves with good food, good words, and truth, we are not tempted to eat junk food, use bad language, or believe false doctrine.

He who blesses his friend with a loud voice,
rising early in the morning, will be counted
a curse to him.
Proverbs 27:14

Be sensitive to those you love, and friends you want to bless, and when. Be sensitive to their needs and feelings. Learn when it is convenient to help them and spend time with them. Otherwise, you may just be irritating. Timing is everything.

Be diligent to know the state of your flocks
and attend to your herds; for riches are not
forever...
Proverbs 27:23

It's great to prosper and enjoy the fruit of our labors, but be mindful to keep doing your best at work. It can all end. Don't slack off.

The wicked flee when no one is chasing them,
but the godly are as bold as lions.
Proverbs 28:1

If you always do the right thing, you never have to fear getting caught doing wrong.

One who increases his possessions by usury and extortion, gathers it for him who will pity the poor.
Proverbs 28:8

If you get money by dishonest means, you will not prosper in the long run. God blesses those who use their increase to help others less fortunate.

Anyone who steals from his father and mother and say, "What's wrong with that?" is no better than a murderer.
Proverbs 28:24

Sin is sin. It all separates you from God. Stealing can be a big temptation, and helping yourself to your parents' goods may seem ok, but unless you ask, it's not. Usually, parents (and grandparents) are glad to give what they've got to their children. So, ask. Give them the joy of giving.

Whoever is a partner with a thief hates his own life.
Proverbs 28:26

Choose your friends wisely. I Corinthians 15:33 says, "Evil company corrupts good morals." Remember, it is easier to pull something down than pull something up.

Whoever stubbornly refuses to accept
criticism will suddenly be destroyed beyond
recovery.
Proverbs 29:1

> Wow! Being able to see our faults humbly is very
> important. Unless we see that we are not perfect, we
> cannot allow God to work in us. Don't be destroyed by
> pride. Let God do His perfect work. Be pliable.

By transgression, an evil man is snared,
but the righteous sings and rejoices.
Proverbs 29:6

> Sin will bring a man down, but following God's
> commands gives us joy and goodness.

The righteous considers the cause of the
poor, but the wicked does not understand
such knowledge.
Proverbs 29:7

> There is a theme here. God reminds us again that
> the Spirit-filled people show compassion to those
> less fortunate. Wicked people are not sensitive to the
> sufferings of others.

If a wise man contends with a foolish man, whether the fool rages or laughs, there is no peace.
Proverbs 29:9

> It's best to walk away from those who cause contention. There's no reasoning with a fool. Words hurt but they don't change who you are. Know you are God's property. He will protect His own.

A fool vents all his feelings, but the wise man holds them back.
Proverbs 29:11

> It is healthy to recognize what your feelings are and what triggers them, but you don't need to express them. Filter your reaction through the Holy Spirit. Self-control is a fruit of the Spirit.

The fear of man brings a snare, but whoever trusts in the Lord shall be safe.
Proverbs 29:25

> There will be times when you will be tempted to compromise on God's Word to please others, but trust God and stand up for His truth. God will strengthen you and bless you.

Every word of God is pure; He is a shield to those who put their trust in Him.
Proverbs 30:5

> We hear so many words of anger, deception, and despair. Don't listen. Look to God's Word for understanding, guidance, and encouragement. This is what builds our faith, which is our shield against Satan's fiery lies.

Remove falsehood and lies from me; give me neither poverty nor riches.
Proverbs 30:8

> This is a prayer. God requires us to be honest with our words. The next part is prayed with understanding that riches can turn your heart from God, and poverty can bring temptation to steal or be dishonest.

Never slander a worker to the employer, or the person will curse you...
Proverbs 30:10

> This is true about the relatives of others. Employers will defend their worker because they represent the company. Instead, make a habit to commend the good workers, and pray for the bad ones. You will be blessed.

The ants are a people not strong, yet they prepare food in summer.
Proverbs 30:25

Ants live just about everywhere, even in climate where winter is freezing. Yet, they survive underground. They take advantage of the summer and gather food for lean times. We too, should learn to set assets aside for future times.

The spider skillfully grasps with its hands, and it is in kings' palaces.
Proverbs 30:28

God gives each of us skills and a job. Do it well and God will open doors.

If you have been foolish in exalting yourself, or if you have devised evil, put your hand to your mouth.
Proverbs 30:32

Don't pretend you have never been prideful or had evil thoughts or spoken badly. It is possible just to stop. You can take control of your mouth and your thoughts.

Do not give your strength to women...It is not for kings to drink wine...
Proverbs 31:3-4

> This chapter is written by a mother warning her son of the destruction of following fleshy desires. Women and alcohol have ruined many lives. Don't allow yourself to fall prey. Run!

Open your mouth for the speechless, in the cause of all who are appointed to die.
Proverbs 31:8

> As Christians, we are to involve ourselves in the world to preserve justice. If we don't, evil will take over. Pray about what God wants you to focus on. Get informed and speak out as God guides.

Who can find a virtuous woman? For her worth is far above rubies.
Proverbs 31:10

> How many men are looking for a moral, modest woman? A woman who loves God is golden. She is worthy of trust because she knows she is accountable to God.

(A virtuous woman) She brings him good and not harm all the days of her life.
Proverbs 31:12

> This is important in marriage, families, and friendships: to always do good for the other, and speak only good of the other. This is true Christian love. It shows you can be trusted.

She also rises while it is yet night, and provides food for her household, And a portion for her maidservants...
Proverbs 31:15-31

> This beautifully describes a selfless woman who sees her purposes for which she is created. She is energetic, wise with money, hardworking, prepares for the future, provides for her family's needs, is charitable, and is kind. Her children will bless her, and God will give her favor. Don't try to do this on your own strength. This is proof that the Spirit of God is in her life.

He has made everything beautiful in its time.
Ecclesiastes 3:11

> This verse gave me hope when I was in deep despair.
> Believe God's Word. Now, I know this is true. From
> brokenness to blessed life. God made all things
> beautiful for me and will for you as you put Him first.

Two are better than one because they have
good reward for their labor. For if they fall,
one lifts his companion.
Ecclesiastes 4:9-10

> We need each other. It's important to learn how to
> be a friend: to help, encourage, be a support to each
> other. As brother and sister, it is even more special.
> God picked you to be lifelong friends.

Do not take to heart everything people say,
lest you hear a servant curse you.
Ecclesiastes 7:21

> This is good advice. First, don't listen in on
> conversations. Second, remember people often say
> things they don't mean. The next verse reminds us that
> we, too, have said things about others we probably
> haven't meant.

Fear God and keep His commandments, For
God will bring every work into judgement.
Ecclesiastes 12:13-14

> These were Solomon's last words after living a life of
> a poet, incredible wealth and pleasure. He realized that
> only what we do for God brings reward. All else is
> empty (vanity).

His banner over me is love.
Song of Solomon 2:4

> Picture yourself at a large banquet. Jesus puts a printed
> banner above that says, "Love." You are special to
> Him, and He wants you and others to know. God
> wants to shower you with blessings and spoil you with
> His love.

You who dwell in the gardens, the companions
listen for your voice.
Song of Solomon 8:13

> Let me hear it!

Cease to do evil, learn to be good: seek justice, rebuke the oppressor, defend the fatherless, plead for the widow.
Isaiah 1:16-17

God is giving some clear instructions. First, turn from evil (anything that is not bringing you closer to God), "Seek" means you are looking or discerning to find what is the right thing to do. Speak up to bullies, help those who are alone like orphans and widows. Don't be passive. Take action for God. You are His hands and mouth.

Woe to those who call evil good and good evil.
Isaiah 5:20

"Woe" means watch out! This is a warning. Don't be persuaded by popular opinion, media or friends, that what the Bible calls sin is acceptable. God has not changed His mind because everyone is doing it. If you are finding yourself in that camp, "woe." Repent and ask God to cleanse you heart and open your eyes to evil. It will spare you much grief.

A virgin will conceive a Son and call His name Immanuel (God with us).
Isaiah 7:14

I love how the Old Testament points to Jesus. There are over three hundred prophecies fulfilled by Jesus. Not coincidences but miraculous completion. We thank God for His word always pointing us to Truth (Jesus).

Behold, God is my salvation. I will trust and not be afraid. For Yah, the Lord, is my strength and my song.
Isaiah 12:2

If you have accepted Jesus' death and shed blood for your sins, you have nothing to fear. You are in God's family. You have God's Spirit living in you to strengthen you and keep you from sin. You have God's presence with you. He is your song of victory. Don't let the devil tell you differently. Sing to God out loud today.

O, Lord, You are my God. I will exalt You.
I will praise Your name, for You have done
wonderful things.
Isaiah 25:1

Before I pray, I like to take time to focus on and thank
God for all He has done for me. The list is endless. If
you do this, the praise and thanksgiving come naturally.

You will keep him in perfect peace, whose
mind is stayed on You because he trusts in
You.
Isaiah 26:3

What robs us of joy, hope, and peace is listening
to anything other than the Word of God instead of
listening for the Holy Spirit daily. Today the news and
circumstances can look dismal, but keep your focus on
God and read His promises. Feed your mind on His
love for you.

For precept must be upon precept, precept upon precept, line upon line, line upon line.
Isaiah 28:10

> This refers to how we study God's Word. You can't just pick and choose what you like. You must study the whole book, God's laws and judgement, how we are to behave, and His wonderful promises and rewards. It makes for peace with God and joy to live.

He gives power to the weak, and to those who have no might, He increase strength.
Isaiah 40:29-31

> But those who wait upon the Lord will renew their strength; They shall mount up with wings like eagles. They shall run and not be weary, they shall walk and not faint.

Fear not, for I am with you; be not dismayed, for I am your God. I will strengthen you., yes, I will help you, I will uphold you with My righteous right hand.
Isaiah 41:10

> Wow! God does it all. He gives us strength, holds us in His hand so we can't fall and wants us to know He is ours. Now, why should we worry about anything? Go to Him instead.

Oh, that you had heeded My commandments! Then your peace would have been like a river, and your righteousness like the waves of the sea.
Isaiah 48:18

What a beautiful picture it is when we follow God's ways. Peace and floating through life like on a gentle wave. Read His Commandments and pray that God teaches you obedience. You will save yourself heartache and despair. They are for your good not punishment. Don't follow popular culture and movies that glamorizes sin. The end is not peace and joy in real life.

Can a woman forget her nursing child and not have compassion on the son of her womb? Surely, they may forget, yet I will not forget you.
Isaiah 49:15

Sometimes it's easy to feel God has forgotten our prayers and needs. As a mother does not forget to feed her helpless baby, God will not forget to supply your needs. He knows when to give you what you need.

All we like sheep have gone astray; We have turned everyone to his own way.
Isaiah 53:6

> God calls us sheep because like sheep we follow the crowd. So much influences what we think and do. That's why we need to read God's Word and let it be our greatest influence. Don't allow yourself to be led by the crowd. We are God's own and need to stand apart from the ungodly thinking and values of today's culture.

Your iniquities have separated you from your God; and your sins have hidden His face from you, so He will not hear,
Isaiah 55:8

> If you feel far from God, search your heart and confess those things that keep God from hearing your prayers. Keep short accounts and stay in communication with your Loving Father.

I will mention the loving kindness of the Lord...according to all He has bestowed on us.
Isaiah 63:7

Those words. loving kindness, describe God's steadfast love, mercy, and faithfulness. To me, it reveals God's endearment to us. We can do nothing to stop His love. So let us freely mention His love and goodness in our conversations and bring praise to His name.

We are the clay you are the potter.
Isaiah 64:8

God is trying to shape you into a beautiful woman or man of God who will show His love and glory to those you meet. Be soft and pliable by listening to the prompting of the Holy Spirit to do what is pleasing to God. His beauty will radiate from you, and God will use you like a vessel that holds water.

Before I formed you in the womb, I knew you.
Jeremiah 1:5

No one's birth is an accident; God had you planned.

For you shall go to all whom I send you and whatever I command you, you shall say.
Jeremiah 1:7

> God 's plan is to use you as His mouth to speak His truth to those who don't know Him.

Break up your fallow ground.
Jeremiah 4:3

> This is a farm instruction, but God is referring to our hearts as hard ground or unreachable. He is saying break it or soften it to be open to His teaching and correcting. Then we will have a fruitful life filled with goodness.

O, Lord correct me with justice, not in Your anger lest you bring me to nothing.
Jeremiah 10:24

> Did you notice yet, that God doesn't let you get away with sin? You may see friends lie, steal, and cheat but God doesn't let you get away with it. He corrects you with justice so you will stay on the Path.

I will bring them back into their land
which I gave to their fathers.
Jeremiah 16:15

> God has promised the land of Israel to the Jewish people. Even today, you are hearing of all the fighting there. Pray for the peace of Jerusalem and God's people. You will be blessed.

Blessed is the man who trusts in the Lord,
and whose hope is in the Lord. For he shall
be like a tree planted by the waters.
Jeremiah 17:7

> Do you want to grow strong and bloom? Trust in God. When you do, you will follow His guidance and you will grow and prosper.

Am I a God near at hand, says the Lord,
and not a God afar off?
Jeremiah 23:23

> Sometimes you'll hear a worship leader say, "Come into the presence of God." Well, you're always in the presence of God; sleeping, eating, studying, playing golf, or baseball. We just need to acknowledge His presence. I think He likes when we do.

For I know the thoughts that I think towards you, thought of good and not of evil, to give you a future and a hope.
Jeremiah 29:11

> God has good plans for you. You can choose to follow or not.

Their souls will be like a watered garden, and they shall sorrow no more at all.
Jeremiah 32:12

> What is more beautiful and refreshing than a watered garden? This is a picture of us when we come to God's Word. It should refresh our souls and as we walk with God. Then we will flourish.

Call on Me and I will answer you, and show you great and mighty things which you do not know.
Jeremiah 33:3

> Don't be timid to ask God to help in big and small problems. He can direct us and reveal solutions that we don't even know are possible. Of course, be ready to listen to His answer.

I will deliver you in that day, says the Lord...
Jeremiah 39:17

Jeremiah prophesied to Israel destruction because of their disobedience. But the servant Ebed Melek will be protected because he put his faith in God. We too, can live under God's umbrella of protection when we trust in Him with all our hearts.

...because you have sinned against the Lord, and have not obeyed the voice of the Lord or walked in His law, in His statutes, or His testimony, therefore this calamity has happened to you.
Jeremiah 44:23

Do you ever wonder why some things go badly? Jeremiah 44-50 contains many prophecies of God's wrath and judgement but tucked in there is vs. 49:11. God shows His compassion and care for children and women who have no husbands. Many times I have experienced His care in tough times.

Many people have been lost sheep. Their shepherds have led them astray.
Jeremiah 50:6

Jeremiah is talking to the Babylonians. Even today, there are many pastors and teachers who lead people astray with false teaching. You need to study God's Word and pray for discernment so you can identify the false teaching and teaching that lines up with God's Word. Don't become a lost sheep or just a follower of the flock. Follow the Shepherd.

The Lord has revealed our righteousness come let us declare in Zion the work of the Lord our God.
Jeremiah 51:10

Jeremiah was declaring the judgement on Babylon but those who were faithful, the righteous would be recognized. We live in a society much like Babylon with materialism, immorality, and selfishness as acceptable. We have the righteousness of Christ if we believe in His atonement for our failures. Let's put off these standards of the world and live as Christ.

His compassions fail not. They are new every morning. Great is Thy faithfulness.
Lamentations 3:22-23

When you are feeling at the end, you have failed, or cannot go on. God has more grace and mercy. He is not done. Every day is filled with strength, compassion and a new start with our loving God.

You, O Lord, remain forever.
Lamentations 5:19

Jeremiah wrote this after the people rejected his warning to repent before God. They suffered judgement. Their lives changed. But God is constant. He is there even when everything around us crumbles or changes.

Go to the house of Israel and speak with My words to them.
Ezekiel 3:4

God was telling Ezekiel to use Scripture when talking to the people. Don't waste your time at a church that doesn't teach straight from the Bible.

Son of man you have seen what the elders of the house of Israel do in the dark...
Ezekiel 8:12

> God sees everything we do and every thought we think. Nothing is hidden. We can't help what comes into our mind sometimes, but we can reject it and not act on it. Don't entertain evil. Entertain God. He is there with you.

I will give them a new spirit and take out the stony heart and give them a heart of flesh that they may walk in My statures. And they shall be my people.
Ezekiel 11:19

> Here God is talking to the Jews in the last days, but we can have this now when we accept Christ as our Savior.
>
> God actually gives you a new Spirit—His Spirit—and a new heart, one that cares about the things He cares about. This is how we can tell if someone is truly Born Again.

The righteousness of the righteous shall be upon himself and the wickedness of the wicked shall be upon himself.
Ezekiel 18:20

> This verse ends the discussion on children paying for the sins of the parents. You may hear this: people teach generational curses. This is false. Ezekiel is settling that here. We are each accountable to God whether we walk with Christ Jesus or not. Our righteousness is in His sacrifice not works or sins of our parents.

Throw away the abominations which are before your eyes, and do not defile yourselves with the idols of Egypt.
Ezekiel 20:7

> Egypt usually refers to our fleshly desire and idols are those things we put before God. There are so many things to lead us away from God today. But God is serious. He said throw it away. Get rid of anything that takes you away from thoughts of God.

They will dwell securely when I execute judgement on those around who despise them.
Ezekiel 28:26

> God is talking about Israel. This prophesy reveals how precious the land of Israel is to God. It is serious that we support this country as a nation and as individuals. God will judge us if we don't.

As my people, they hear your words, but they do not do them; for with their mouth, they show much love, but with their hearts pursue their own gain.
Ezekiel 33:31

> God is talking to Ezekiel. Some people look nice, say they love God, but they don't fool Him. God sees our hearts and our motivation. Ask Him to give you a heart that pursues God, not your own gain.

I will take the heart of stone out of your flesh and give you a heart of flesh. I will put My Spirit within you and cause you to walk in my statutes...
Ezekiel 36:26-27

There we have it. When you surrender your life to God, He gives you a caring, loving heart. Then, He gives you His Holy Spirit to empower you to walk according to His laws. You will lose your interest in worldly pleasures. Your fulfillment comes from God. This is the Christian life.

Surely, I will cause breath to enter into you, and you shall live.
Ezekiel 37:4

This is in the story of dry bones. God brought them to life again. But look at how. God breathed. Without breath we have no life. For spiritual life, we need God's breath, which is the Holy Spirit. And notice, the dry bones did nothing. God did all the work. Ask Him to breath His life into you today and see how you come alive.

His voice was like the sound of many waters and the earth shone with His glory.
Ezekiel 43:2

Ezekiel had this vision. God's voice was like the sound of many waters. Next time you go to the beach meditate on that. Maybe that's why I feel at peace there by the water. I don't think taking a shower does the same.

They shall wear linen. They shall not clothe themselves with anything that causes sweat.
Ezekiel 44:18

This is instruction to the priests who teach and worship. Our service and worship should not be hard work causing sweat, but it should be pleasant and easy because it is generated by the Holy Spirit.

At the end of ten days, their features appeared better and fatter in flesh than all the young men who are the king's delicacies.
Daniel 1:15

> This is referring to Daniel and his friends who fasted on veggies and water and refused to eat the king's meat and wine. Daniel put his faith in God and proved that it was God who would strengthen him, not an expensive diet. Test Him like Daniel. Don't follow popular trends but trust God to be your coach to guide you and give you strength.

Daniel distinguished himself above the governors and satraps, because an excellent spirit was in him; and the king set Daniel over the whole realm.
Daniel 6:3

> There are many books written on how to succeed, but Daniel had the real secret. He stayed strong in the Lord by prayer, fasting, and obeying God. "An excellent spirit" was in him. That is the Spirit of God. That is what makes us attractive and successful.

I set my face toward the Lord God to make by prayer and supplication with fast in sackcloth and ashes.
Daniel 9:3

> Daniel didn't just give a speed prayer before eating. This was a deliberate and humble entrance to the throne of God. Daniel confessed his sin and then spoke of his need. We are able to come before a holy God because we are cleansed by Christ's blood. Always be humble enough to search your heart and confess your shortcomings, then God will forgive your sin and hear your prayer.

Go your way till the end; for you shall rest, and will arise to your inheritance at the end of the days.
Daniel 12:13

> We who have forgiveness in Christ Jesus can go through life in peace knowing that in the end, we have a great inheritance with Jesus. We are guaranteed the same as Him, and He is a king.

My people perish for lack of knowledge.
Hosea 4:5

Hosea was getting on the priests for not teaching the Word of God. We need not waste our time at churches that entertain, but stick to a church that teaches through the Bible. You should be diligent and don't wait for others to feed you. Pick a book from the Bible and read through it.

Sow for yourselves righteousness; Reap in mercy; Break up your fallow ground.
Hosea 10:12

When we sow righteousness, it means to obey the Spirit. Plant goodness, kindness, and self-control. Break up fallow ground means to search your heart for those areas you are keeping from God. You know, holding onto behavior or thoughts you know are wrong. Be honest and humble. God wants to soften your heart to Him so He can develop spiritual fruit in your life.

Return to the Lord your God, for you have stumbled because of your iniquity.
Hosea 14:1

> Did you ever have a time when nothing seemed to be going right? Maybe it's because you're not going God's way. Repent or turn from iniquity or sin and return to God and His Word for guidance.

I will restore to you the years that the locusts have eaten.
Joel 2:25

> Sin is like a locust. It takes away our strength, joy, and blessings. But when we repent— confess and put away our sinful habit, God will restore our relationship and give a new start.

Can two walk together unless they agree?
Amos 3:3

> Many people think they are good with God, but unless they submit to His will and follow Him, they are not in agreement. Pray daily for guidance. Read the Word of God, and you will learn how to walk with the living God. I would rather walk with God than anybody else.

I will bring back the captives of My people Israel.
Amos 9:14

The book of Amos has many hard prophesies about God's judgement in the end times. The goodness of God is on us who are saved by faith in Jesus. He is also talking about His favor to the nation Israel. God will bring the Jews who are scattered back their homeland to live.

But on Mount Zion shall be deliverance and there shall be holiness.
Obadiah 1:17

Take our one-chapter book about God's judgement on Edom, the descendants of Esau. The Edomites were violent and hostile to their cousins, the Israelites. God judged them as they treated others. God's judgement was used to cleanse and purify. What was left was beauty and holiness.

The word of the Lord came a second time saying, "Arise and go to Nineveh."
Jonah 3:1

God always gives us another chance to obey Him and be blessed. Jonah thought he could run from God, but God caught him by using a big fish and brought him back to Joppa to try again. Let's keep this in mind when we try to ignore God's instruction. Like Jonah, we may be asked to love and be kind to someone we are mad at. Just do it the first time God asks.

He has shown you, O man, what is good; and what the Lord requires of you: about to do justly (fairly), to love mercy (give kindness where it is not deserved), and to walk humbly with your God.
Micah 6:8

When you want to know God's will for you, here you have it: Be just, show mercy, and be humble.

Your injury has no healing, your wound is severe.
Nahum 3:19

These words of hopelessness were to the city of Nineveh. 150 years after God sent Jonah to save them, the people left their love of God and reverted back to sinful ways. God gives us all many chances to repent and follow him. But if we keep returning to sin, He will leave us.

The just shall live by faith.
Habakkuk 2:4

Everything was grim in Judah at this time. The Babylonians were taking over. Habakkuk did not despair. He had faith that God was in control and would take care. We are living in a time when unbelievably evil ideas are considered good. We may be ridiculed for our faith, but know that God has a purpose even when evil is strong. You stay even stronger in your faith in God. God never fails.

He will rejoice over you with gladness...He will delight on you with shouts of joy.
Zephaniah 3:17

> This is speaking of Israel after God's judgement. We became part of this family when we accepted Jesus as our redeemer. So just imagine how you will feel when God Rejoices over you and shouts for joy.

And the Lord said to Satan, "The Lord rebuke you, Satan."
Zechariah 3:2

> Zechariah had a vision of the high priest rebuilding the temple, and the devil standing in the way. As you grow spiritually, pray to discern the devil's attempts to stop you from doing God's will. And speak out, "The Lord rebuke you!" You will be amazed when you experience the power of God defend you.

Not by might nor my power, but by my Spirit.
Zechariah 4:6

Zerubbabel had an overwhelming task in rebuilding the temple. The prophet gave this message. We, too, need to be reminded that it is God's Spirit that changes us and gives us the power to do big things for Him. What is overwhelming you? Ask God to take control.

These things you shall do: Speak the truth to your neighbor; Give judgement for truth, justice, and peace; Let none of you think evil in your heart against your neighbor; and do not love a false oath. For these things I hate.
Zechariah 8:16

It must be important to obey these commands. It sends a chill up my spine reading the last sentence...for these things God hates. I sure don't want to do what God hates.

"What are those wounds between your arms?" Then he will answer, "those with which I was wounded in the house of my friends."
Zechariah 13:6

This was a message to the prophets in the last days, who will be ashamed of His vision because it is not popular.

This prophesy is about Jesus being betrayed by His friends at the end. They ran off and denied Him. It hurts to have a friend betray you. It will happen... Jesus knows this very well.

"I have no pleasure in you," says the Lord of hosts, "Nor will I accept an offering from your hands."
Malachi 1:10

These words seem very harsh, but God is looking at our hearts. When we give or do things for God, He looks at our hearts or motivations. We are to do all things out of love for God.

New Testament

The Spirit of God descended like a dove, alighted upon Jesus. And suddenly a voice from heaven said, "This is my beloved Son, in whom I am well pleased."
Mathew 3:16-17

This is an important passage. First, it teaches we need to be baptized with the water and with the Holy Spirit. Let Him come into your life and take control. Lay down your desires, and let God wash and renew your heart. It also teaches that God is three separate persons as we see the Son, the Holy Spirit, and the Father.

Seek first the kingdom of God and His righteousness, and all these things will be added to you.
Mathew 6:33

Jesus was teaching us to trust God for all our needs. God is a good father and will not leave us naked or hungry. He wants us to put Him first and cherish our relationship with Him above all else. I can testify of many times God miraculously provided for me and my daughter.

...by their fruits you will know them.
Mathew 7:20

In this chapter, Jesus tells us not to judge others lest we be judged. Meaning we shouldn't condemn someone for their sin as we are sinners too, forgiven by God's grace. But we are to be fruit inspectors, especially in pastors and picking close friends. We are to look for the fruits of the Spirit which are: love, joy, peace, long suffering, kindness, patience, goodness, faithfulness, gentleness, and self-control. It is the Holy Spirit that produces these in our lives. If you don't have these, pray for the Spirit to grow them in your life.

Be wise as serpents and innocent as doves.
Mathew 10:16

Jesus is talking to His disciples about persecution for their beliefs. We will also encounter this. Jesus' advice is to use wisdom (shun evil, cling to that which is good). And recognize useless conversation and evil doings and like the serpent, slither away. Don't retaliate, but like a dove, speak peace and gentleness. You can't fight evil in the flesh. Let God fight those battles for you.

Peter had come down out of the boat. He walked on water to go to Jesus.
Mathew 14:29

This is stated so simply. Jesus told Peter to come, and without questioning, Peter obeyed and miraculously walked on water to Jesus. I think we, too, could do miraculous things if we would obey and trust the prompting of the Holy Spirit to step out. Also, Peter never took his eyes off Jesus. When he did, Peter sank. Keep your eyes on God, not on doubt or distrust.

Where two or three are gathered together in My name, I am there.
Matthew 18:19

We know God is always with us, but there is power in prayer with other believers. When you can pray together, God likes that and wants to be part of the group. He promises His Spirit will be there.

Go into the village and find a donkey tied with her colt. Loose and bring them to Me. If anyone asks, say, "The Lord has need of them."
Matthew 21:2

Jesus tells two disciples to go to town and directs them to take someone's property, like that would be just fine. The Holy Spirit works before we even get to where we are going. Jesus knew where the donkeys were, and that the Holy Spirit had already spoke to the owner that someone would come for them. When God sends you out, He has already made preparations.

You shall love the Lord your God with all your heart, with all your soul, and all your mind...And love your neighbor as yourself.
Matthew 22:37

Those Pharisees and Sadducees were trying to trip Jesus up and wanted Him to describe the greatest law from the Ten Commandments. He did not pick a law but made it simple. If you love God and love others, then all the laws are obeyed. It just falls into place.

But first, put God in your heart and mind and let His Spirit fill your soul. Then this extraordinary love will take over.

And lo, I am with you always, even to the end of the age.
Matthew 28:20

These are Jesus' last words to His disciples. They are words for us to know and keep in our hearts. There have been times of fear, loneliness, and disappointment, but I have always been comforted that Jesus has been with me through it all. I am never alone.

Whoever does the will of God is My brother and My sister and mother.
Mark 3:35

Jesus was making the point that when we put our faith in Him and obey God's commands, we enter into a close family relationship with Him. Imagine, we are part of Jesus' family.

Whatever enter a man from the outside cannot defile him. What comes out of a man defiles him.
Mark 7:20

The Jews had strict dietary laws, and Jesus is saying, "God isn't looking at how you keep the laws, but what is the condition of your heart." Are you doing things out of love for Him, or to earn favor by following man-made laws? God looks at the heart.

Whoever desires to become great among you shall be your servant.
Mark 10:43

> Jesus spent His whole life comforting, teaching, healing, and showing up for others. Here He is telling His disciples great people are not the big shots who get everyone to jump and serve Him, but those whose heart want to help and give to others. God likes these people.

Whatever things you ask when you pray, believe that you will receive them, and you will have them.
Mark 11:24

> So much has been written about prayer. It is our all-important connection to God. Now He knows our needs, our thoughts, and our heartaches, but He wants us to come to Him as we would a loving father. He wants to build our bond of faith and trust. Nothing is more joyful than answered prayer; knowing God heard and cared.

"Sit here while I pray."
Mark 14:32

Jesus is our example. He was facing a sure and cruel death, but He still prayed, "not my will, but what You will."

That is what God wants for us; to be willing to pray for His will in our lives, not pray just to fulfill our earthly desires. And why not? His will is perfect because He knows us perfectly.

For with God nothing is impossible.
Luke 1:37

The angel Gabriel was telling Mary that God was to use her, and she did not need to worry about how it would come about. When you yield yourself to God, He will take care of the details. Ask Him to lead you to do His will. Nothing is impossible.

Love your enemies, do good to those who hate you, bless those who curse you, and pray for those who spitefully use you.
Luke 6:27

This is a tough order. It is not what we naturally feel like doing. But that is the point, "It is no longer I who live, but Christ lives in me." Start by obeying and do what doesn't come naturally— be kind to your enemy. Eventually this will be natural.

I say to you, her sins, which are many, are forgiven, for she loved much.
Luke 7:47

Jesus is honoring the woman who anointed His feet with oil. She was so full of gratitude and love receiving God's forgiveness for her sin, she became a new creation. Let's remember to confess our faults and receive that forgiveness and be filled with that joy of God.

Seek first the Kingdom of God and all these things shall be added.
Luke 12:31

This is one verse that I stood on for many years. Jesus was the Kingdom of God. He told His disciples not to worry about food, clothes and their needs. He just told them that God counts the hairs of their heads. He knows everything about you and wants to provide miraculously, but you need to put Him first. Talk with Him first. Ask Him to take care of you because you trust Him above all else.

Whoever exalts himself will be humbled, and who humbled himself will be exalted.
Luke 14:11

Jesus told His friends when they come into a room, don't take the best seat. You might be asked to move. Always let others exalt you. God wants us to have humility.

Receive your sight; your faith has made you well.
Luke 18:42

The blind man cried out to Jesus for mercy believing that He could heal him. His faith preceeded the miracle. Don't be afraid to ask for the impossible. Trust God and your faith will be rewarded.

Jesus looked up and saw Zacchaeus (he was in a tree), and Jesus said, "Come down, for today I must stay at your house."
Luke 19:5

Jesus got ridiculed for being friends with a tax collector (a sinner, a cheater, etc.). This is comforting to me. I need not be ashamed of the sins of my past. Jesus wants me for a friend too, because I sought Him and put my faith in Him.

Then Satan entered Judas, called Iscariot, who was numbered among the Twelve.
Luke 22:3

I don't know about you, but this sends shivers down my spine. How could you walk, talk, and eat with Jesus and then let Satan enter your life and follow him? It happens though, little by little. Be careful what you listen to, what you read and who you spend your time with. Don't let Satan enter your life.

He (Jesus) said to them, "Have you any food?"
Luke 24:41

Now, this may seem like an odd scripture for Easter, but this took place after Jesus was torn apart, nailed to the cross, and pierced in the heart with a sword and buried. Now He's walking around and wants to eat. We have a living God. Seen by many, walking and talking in a human body after death. He is a real person today. Ask Jesus to make Himself real to you.

For God so loved the world that He gave His only begotten Son, that whoever believes in Him should not perish but have everlasting life.
John 3:16

This was the answer Jesus gave to Nicodemus when he asked how he could be born a second time. When we surrender our lives to Jesus, we get a spiritual birth. You come alive by God's Spirit. You are born a second time. You hear and see things from a new perspective... God's.

I am the bread of life. He who comes to Me shall never hunger, and he who believes Me shall never thirst.
John 6:35

Jesus is saying that we hunger spiritually for truth and meaning in our lives. Knowing Jesus and who we are (God's children), gives us belonging and meaning. We are spiritually full and satisfied.

Whoever commits sin is a slave of sin...If the Son makes you free, you will be free indeed.
John 8:34-35

> Sin often looks fun or cool. That's why it is tempting. But once we do it; (lie, cheat, drugs, immoral sex,) we become accustomed and addicted to this behavior. When Jesus forgives us, the Holy Spirit gives us the power to break that control and change our will. You are free indeed, but you must choose.

Many believed in Him, but because of the Pharisees they did not confess Him...for they loved the praise of men more than the praise of God.
John 12:42-43

> You may have to choose one day whether to look like a dork to friends and confess your faith in Jesus and the Bible or be accepted by them and take part in their godless talk and activities. Whose praise is more valuable to you, man or God's?

*You did not choose Me, but I chose you...
you are to bear much fruit...whatever you
ask in My name, the Father will give you.
Love one another.*
John 15:16-17

I simplified these verses so we could clearly see what is said. God Chose you. He likes you. You are to stay in the Word and follow God's commands. That's how you bear the fruits of the Spirit. Now, if you do when you pray in Jesus' name, God will answer. Wow! That is a fact.

Then we are told to love each other. That means everybody, even the mean, cruel, and stinky. The secret is to stay focused on God's truth and bask in His love.

*Now the servants and officers made a fire
and stood there and warmed themselves.
And Peter stood with them and warmed
himself.*
John 18:18

When things go wrong or life gets tough, it is easy to go to worldly comfort of solutions (cheating, lying, drugs, alcohol). These are the enemy fires. Keep your faith in God to help you. His ways are not man's ways. You will experience amazing results.

Then, as soon as they had come to land, they saw a fire of coals there, and fish laid on it and bread.
John 21:9

This is a scene after Jesus' death. He appeared to His disciples and had them cast their nets where the fish were. Then, we see the sweetness of His care. Before they came back to shore, Jesus prepared food for the disciples. Not only did they reap the abundance of the fish by obeying His word, but they experienced Jesus going beyond the obvious and preparing for their immediate needs.

He will care for all your needs too. Obey Him, Trust Him.

You shall receive power when the Holy Spirit has come upon you...
Acts 1:8

The Holy Spirit is a person. The one who comes to us now to teach, comfort, and guide. You may believe in God and know about Jesus, but you need the Holy Spirit daily to be present with you. Ask Him to come upon you like a mighty rushing wind (Acts 2:2) so you might know Him.

And Stephen, full of faith and power, did great wonders and signs among the people.
Acts 6:8

> In Chapter 5, we learned that Stephen was picked to serve and wait on tables (like at Chick-Fil-A). He used this as an opportunity to speak the Word and pray for healing with those he served. We should share our faith wherever we go. God will use you. Be aware. Be available.

And Simon saw that through the laying on of the apostles' hands the Holy Spirit was given, he offered them money to receive this power.
Acts 8:18

> Simon was a sorcerer (magician). He saw the power of God manifested in healings and thought it was a trick he could use. His faith was not in the power of God, and he thought he could use this deception to make money. Pray for wisdom and discernment. There are still charlatans today who use deception to prey on Christians.

Paul and Barnabas were persecuted and thrown out of the city. They were filled with joy and the Holy Spirit.
Acts 13:50,52

This is almost comical. Paul and Barnabas were thrown out of Antioch for preaching about Jesus' death and resurrection. Most of us would feel angry and humiliated. Not these two. They were joyful because their preaching was effective, and angered those who opposed the Gospel.

At midnight Paul and Silas were praying and singing hymns to God, and the prisoners were listening to them.
Acts 16:25

Prior to this, Paul and Silas were stripped, beaten with rods, and put in stocks. Now they are singing and praising God. Praise and worship are not time wasters, but real acts of worship and connecting with God. Look what followed in verse 26. There was an earthquake, the prison doors opened, and their chains fell loose. Next time you're feeling low, sing to God and expect Him to show up.

It is more blessed to give than to receive.
Acts 20:36

> Before Paul left Ephesus, he quoted Jesus. These
> words don't ring true until you put them into practice.
> We are a culture of indulgence like never before. Try
> giving to others before you indulge yourself. You will
> be surprised.

Now as he reasoned about righteousness,
self-control, and judgement to come, Felix
was afraid and answered, "Go away for
now; when I have a more convenient time,
I will call for you."
Acts 24:25

> Paul was brought before Felix, the governor, and
> shared his testimony and all about Christ. Felix was
> convicted by the Holy Spirit, which is why he was
> afraid. But he wasn't ready to repent of his sin and
> change his life. Many people hear the Gospel and feel
> God's love, but they don't want to leave their sinful
> ways. They are passing on eternal life for a lie (sin is
> better than God's blessing).

Paul dwelt two whole years in his own rented house, and received all who came to him, preaching the kingdom of God and teaching Jesus Christ with confidence, no one forbidding him.
Acts 28:30-31

> This is the end of the book of Acts. Paul in chains under house arrest. Free rent and everyone could freely come and hear him preach. Also, it gave him time to write the letters to the Ephesians, Philippians, and Philemon and the Colossians. Men tried to punish Paul, but God used it for His purposes.

For all have sinned and fall short of the glory of God.
Romans 3:23

> This is why everyone needs Jesus' sacrifice for redemption. It is God's grace. He did all the work. We just have to say yes (I believe) and Amen (I agree with God).

Having been set free from sin, you become slaves of righteousness.
Romans 6:18

> A slave is in bondage to obey the master. Sin of all kinds is addictive, and you feel you can't stop. You are enslaved. But the love of God and the power of Jesus' atonement breaks all bondage. Now you are a slave to live pure and godly lives. You can't help it. That is when you know God's Spirit has taken control. Give Him permission.

For those who live according to the flesh, set their minds on the things of the flesh, but those who live according to the Spirit, have their minds set on the things of the Spirit.
Romans 8:5

> Many times, God reminds us that what we think about guides our actions. Do you want to be angry, selfish, lustful? Listen to what popular culture tells you is ok. But if you want to walk in peace, get your mind on Jesus. Read the word, pray. Verse 6 says "to be spiritually minded is life and peace." I want that!

Repay no one evil for evil
Romans 12:17

Do not be overcome by evil, but overcome evil with good.
Romans 12:21

These two scriptures point out that there is evil. We will encounter evil in many forms and often through the words and actions of others. To overcome (get rid of the oppression of the devil), repay evil with kindness, patience, generosity. If evil attacks, and it brings out godliness in us, we win. The devil loses and will back off.

Put on the Lord Jesus Christ and make no provision for the flesh to fulfill its lust.
Romans 13:14

I love this image. As Christians, we are to be changing daily to be more like Jesus. Each morning, get dressed, but don't go out without putting on your Jesus suit so you will look, and act more like Him.

Do you not know you are the temple of God and that the Spirit of God dwells in you?
1 Corinthians 3:16

When I went to Italy, we saw many magnificent cathedrals with artwork, embellished with gold. But God doesn't live in those garish buildings. His Spirit dwells in our frail bodies. Be aware of His presence and desire to be empowered to live for the glory of God.

Do not be deceived. Neither fornicators, idolaters, no adulterers, nor homosexual nor sodomites, not thieves, nor covetous, nor drunkards, nor revilers, nor extortioners will inherit the kingdom of God.
1 Corinthians 6:9

This is quite a list. Before this statement, Paul reminds us that we are not to judge unbelievers because they have no knowledge of right and wrong. But this scripture is to the believer. We know what God wants for us, and we have the power to say, "no." Don't let movies and celebrities fool you with bad behavior. It will lead to your destruction and separation from God.

Love suffers long and is kind; love does not envy; love does not parade itself; is not puffed up; does not behave rudely, does not seek its own, is not provoked, thinks no evil; does not rejoice in iniquity, but rejoices in truth; bears all things, believes all things, hope all things, endures all things. Love never fails.
1 Corinthians 13:4

Now, put your name in place of the word "love." How are you doing?

Do not be deceived. "Evil company corrupts good habits."
1 Corinthians 15:33

As you both start out this school year, you have a wonderful opportunity to make new friends. Be friendly, kind, and smile. But pray for wisdom and discernment. Stay away from those whose values are not godly, and who have habits that are not edifying (smoking, vaping, immorality). It will bring you down. Let God's Spirit guide you.

Let all you do be done in love.
1 Corinthians 16:14

> Love should be your motivation for all you do.

And we, who with unveiled faces all reflect the Lord's glory, are being transformed into his likeness with ever-increasing glory, which comes from the Lord, who is Spirit.
11 Corinthians 3:18

> We are becoming more like Christ all the time by the Spirit working in us. Spend time with Him. You have access; that is the meaning of "unveiled faces." What a privilege.

Now then we are ambassadors for Christ...
11 Corinthians 5:20

> Did you know that is who you are? An ambassador is a representative in a foreign country. We speak for and represent Jesus on Earth, but this is not our real home. Let people know who He is by your words and actions.

He who sows sparingly will reap sparingly, and he who sows bountifully will reap bountifully. Give not grudgingly for God loves a cheerful giver.
II Corinthians 9:6-7

> Now this is comparing our financial giving to ministry to planting seed. You plant few seeds; you get few crops. But God wants us to give generously with love and faith, and He will reward us generously.

Examine yourselves as to whether you are in the faith. Test yourselves. Do you not know that Jesus Christ is in you?
II Corinthians 13:5

> Being in the faith means living what you believe. Paul is saying if you have Jesus living in you, then you should live like it.

The law (The Ten Commandments) was put in charge to lead us to Christ that we might be justified by faith.
Galatians 3:24

> God gave the Ten Commandments so we would learn what a holy life is like. But He gave us Jesus to atone for the fact that we don't live up to all that. We are sinners. We put our faith in Christ, and we are justified (made righteous). Don't hang your head in shame, but rejoice. You are accepted into God's family. The law pointed out your need for Christ.

Let us not grow weary in doing good, for in due season we shall reap if we don't lose heart. As we have opportunity, let us do good to all.
Galatians 6:9-10

> So much as we grow up doesn't seem fair. Living here can be hard: work, school, chores.
>
> But we will reap the benefits if we don't give up. Most of all, God wants you to look for ways to help others. Try to help someone every day.

Now, therefore, you are no longer strangers and foreigners, but fellow citizens with the saints and members of the household of God. Ephesians 2:19

Do you ever feel like you don't fit in? You don't, because as a child of God, the ways of these earthlings are not what God puts in our hearts. We are citizens of Heaven. We are members of God's family. Rejoice that you don't fit in when others are practicing ungodly behavior and calling it good.

Walk circumspectly, not as fools but as wise, redeeming the time, because the days are evil. Ephesians 5:15

This is telling us to choose our behavior and pursue it carefully. Also, follow God's wisdom—not to is foolish. Use your time for good. There are so many things to distract us and lead us in the wrong direction.

Finally, my brethren, whatever things are true, whatever things are noble, whatever things are just, whatever things are pure, whatever things are lovely, whatever things are of good report, if there is any virtue and if there is anything praiseworthy, meditate on these things.
Philippians 4:8

The book of Philippians has a lot of good advice on how to live with joy. Forget about past hurts and mistakes; stay focused on God's calling for you: pray about everything big and small. And here is how you can stay joyful...think on these things. Don't waste time on trash, lies, or evil.

Let your speech always be with grace, seasoned with salt, that you may know how you ought to answer each one.
Colossians 4:6

Our words should be "always" gracious. That is showing undeserved kindness. No bad language or smart remarks. Seasoned with salt; preserve, in this case, the truth.

Aspire to lead a quiet life, to mind your own business and to work with your own hands.
1 Thessalonians 4:11

> My dad used to say, "Mind your own business." He was right. If you follow these rules, you will have peace and lack nothing.

If anyone will not work, neither shall he eat.
II Thessalonians 3:10

> God's plan is that we work and earn and rejoice that God enables us to do that. People who are lazy or complain about work do not have gratitude. They will never feel fulfilled.

I desire that men pray everywhere lifting up holy hands...that women adorn themselves in modest apparel not with gold or pearls or costly clothing.
1 Timothy 2:8

> This is pretty clear how God wants you to act as a man or woman of God. He wants our focus on Him, not what others think.

Godliness with contentment is great gain.
1 Timothy 6:6

> There's nothing wrong with working hard at school, work, or sports. But most of all, pursue godly attitude and behavior. This brings contentment.

Let no one despise your youth, be an example to the believers in word, in conduct, in love, in spirit, in faith, in purity.
1 Timothy 4:12

> Be an example to old legalistic Christians that age doesn't determine your relationship with God. Daniel was a strong man of faith from the time he was a young teenager.

God has not given us the spirit of fear, but of power, and love, and a sound mind.
II Timothy 1:7

> People fear when they can't understand or control something.
>
> We need not fear anything because we know God is in control, He has given us the power to overcome evil, and strength to endure hardship. We have His love even when we fail. God guides our thoughts when we focus on Him.

Be subject to rulers and authorities to obey, to be ready for every good work, to speak evil of no one, to be peaceable gentle showing humility to all men.
Titus 3:1

As believers we are to obey laws and even traffic rules because God commands us. Do good quickly, check your words. We are to be kind and at peace. Let the Spirit of God be in control. Let go and watch how He can change you.

Confident of your obedience, I write to you, knowing you will do even more than I ask.
Philemon 1:21

Paul wrote this to his friend. To receive someone's confidence that you will do more than asked is a compliment. I do pray we all do our best in every situation. And don't hesitate to express your confidence in others as well.

*The Word of God is living and powerful
and sharper than a two-edged sword.
Hebrews 4:12*

Just as a sword can cut and separate flesh from bone,
God's Word can help us separate good from evil, truth
from lies, God's guidance for our decisions. Read
the Word, search for truth, and apply it to your every
situation.

*He lives to make intercession for them (those
who are saved).
Hebrews 7:25*

This is so comforting and humbling to think Jesus is
praying for me. Sometimes I don't know how to pray,
but He does. He knows my needs better than I do.

*And let us consider one another in order to
stir up love and good works.
Hebrews 10:24*

God is always reminding us to put the welfare of others
before our own. In this case, to encourage love (by
giving love) and encourage someone to go God's way.

Lay aside every weight and sin which ensnares us, and run with endurance the race set before you.
Hebrews 12:1

> Your race is to please God and let Him guide your path. He has set you up for success, but don't get involved in practices and activities that ensnare or defeat you. Run this race like an athlete; stay focused on God and doing good, and you will succeed.

Faith without works is dead.
James 2:20

> We are not saved because we do good deeds but because our faith is in God's sacrifice for our sin. We enter into a love relationship with God. And the evidence of His love in our lives should bring about a change in us. We should love others, care for them as God does. This is evidence of our faith.

Submit to God. Resist the devil and he will flee from you. Draw near to God and He will draw near to you.
James 4:7-8

This is how you can choose to do the right thing even when it's tempting not to. Resist. Draw near or call on God. You know how you feel when your cats come near and rub on you? We like it. So does God. Draw near to Him.

Be ready to give a defense to everyone who asks you a reason for the hope that is in you.
1 Peter 3:15

Hopefully, our lives do look different from the majority of our culture. Living a moral, unselfish life is not the norm. But if you are asked why you don't indulge yourself in worldly pleasures, can you say why? As you read God's Word, ask the Holy Spirit to teach how to reply. What is your relationship to God based on? I hope it is love and knowing God is real.

Cast all your care upon Him, for He cares for you.
1 Peter 5:7

> What do you worry about? Talk to God about it and ask Him to take care of it. God knows all your needs and desires, and He wants the best for you. You can trust in Him.

Grow in grace and knowledge of our Lord and Savior Jesus Christ.
II Peter 3:18

> Peter ends his letter to Christians with these words. He's warning them about false teaching and becoming in bondage to sin.
>
> Spend time in God's Word, pray and meditate on His goodness, and you will grow in grace and knowledge of Jesus.

Love one another, for love is of God.
1 John 4:7

He who does not love, does not know God.
1 John 4:8

> Pray for those who don't love but react with irritation or anger. They need to know Jesus.

He loved us and sent His Son to be a propitiation for our sin.
1 John 4:9

That word propitiation means that Jesus took the punishment we deserved so God would not punish us.

No one has seen God at any time. If we love one another, God abides in us, and His love is perfected in us.
1 John 4:12

Letting God love others through us is how others come to know God exists. God uses us for good. What a privilege. This is humbling to know, and it is hard to comprehend. As believers in Jesus, God lives in us. No one has seen God, but they see us. We bring His love to them.

If we ask anything according to His will, He hears us.
1 John 5:14

Wow! You can ask God anything, and He hears you. But remember, He only answers according to His will.

For many deceivers have gone out into the world who do not confess Jesus Christ as coming in the flesh.
II John 7

> You will meet people who say they believe like you do in Jesus. Unless they believe He was a man born of a virgin, died for your sin, and came back again in the flesh, they are not talking about the same God. John warns us not to even invite such a one into our house.

Keep yourself in the love of God.
Jude 2:1

> God wanted to bless your life. You need to be walking with Him, obeying, and trusting Him. Then you will be in the place where you will receive all He has for you. I know I missed out on many blessings walking outside of His will.

As many as I love, I rebuke and chasten. Therefore, be zealous and repent.
Revelation 3:19

> Did you ever notice that you can't get away with doing wrong? If you are God's child, He isn't going to let you get away with bad behavior. So just confess and repent. He loves you too much to let you sin.

Twenty-four elders fell down before the Lamb, each with a harp and golden bowls full of incense.
Revelation 5:8

> Here John is describing his vision in the past tense, but this is future. The bowls of incense represent the prayers of saints (us). Every time you pray, you are sending up a sweet fragrance to God.

God shall wipe away every tear from their eyes.
Revelation 7:17

> There will be 144,000 Jews who come to Christ during the Tribulation. They will have suffered much, but these words are sweet; "God shall wipe away their tears."
>
> He will wipe away yours too. Go to Him for comfort when things get tough.

They overcame him (the devil) by the blood of the Lamb and the word of their testimony.
Revelation 12:11

> To get temptation and the devil off your back, speak out that you are covered by the blood of Christ, and you believe He is Lord and Savior.

Anyone not found in the Book of Life was cast into the lake of fire.
Revelation 20:15

> If you don't want to swim in fire for eternity, make sure your name is in that book. Confess Jesus as Lord and Savior. Know Him and who He is. Obey Him. Make sure He is Lord of your life.

There shall be no more death, nor sorrow, nor crying. There shall be no more pain, for the former things have passed away. Behold I make all things new.
Revelation 21:4–5

> God is going to create a new Heaven and Earth where we will live in His presence. All things will be as He planned. We can do our best to accept His love and follow His guidance until that day.

This is the end of God's love letter to you.